DEMOCRATIC AUTHORITY
AND
THE SEPARATION OF CHURCH AND STATE

DEMOCRATIC AUTHORITY
AND
THE SEPARATION OF
CHURCH AND STATE

Robert Audi

OXFORD
UNIVERSITY PRESS

OXFORD
UNIVERSITY PRESS

Oxford University Press, Inc., publishes works that further
Oxford University's objective of excellence
in research, scholarship, and education.

Oxford   New York

Auckland   Cape Town   Dar es Salaam   Hong Kong   Karachi
Kuala Lumpur   Madrid   Melbourne   Mexico City   Nairobi
New Delhi   Shanghai   Taipei   Toronto

With offices in

Argentina   Austria   Brazil   Chile   Czech Republic   France   Greece
Guatemala   Hungary   Italy   Japan   Poland   Portugal   Singapore
South Korea   Switzerland   Thailand   Turkey   Ukraine   Vietnam

Published by Oxford University Press, Inc.
198 Madison Avenue, New York, New York 10016

www.oup.com

Library of Congress Cataloging-in-Publication Data
Audi, Robert
Democratic authority and the separation of church and state / Robert Audi.
p.   cm.
Includes bibliographical references (p.   ) and index.
ISBN 978-0-19-979608-3 (alk. paper)
1. Democracy—Religious aspects. 2. Religion and state. I. Title.
BL65.P7A82   2011
201'.72—dc22   2010042452

1 3 5 7 9 8 6 4 2

Printed in the United States of America
on acid-free paper

CONTENTS

Preface and Acknowledgments vii

Introduction 3

1. The Autonomy of Ethics and the Moral Authority of
   Religion 9
     I. The Autonomy of Ethics 11
     II. Moral Knowledge: General and Particular 13
     III. Religion, Theology, and Ethics 15
     IV. Theoethical Equilibrium: The Integration of Religion
       and Ethics 20
     V. Divine Command Ethics and Secular Morality 25

2. The Liberty of Citizens and the Responsibilities of
   Government 37
     I. The Separation of Church and State and the Limits of
       Democratic Authority 39
     II. The Liberty Principle and the Scope of Religious
       Freedom 40
     III. The Equality Principle and the Case against
       Establishment 43
     IV. The Neutrality Principle: Accommodationist
       Secularity 45

V. Religious Neutrality, Valuational Neutrality,
and Public Policy 48

3. The Secular State and the Religious Citizen 59
I. Freedom of Expression in the Advocacy of Laws
and Public Policies 59
II. Major Principles Governing the Advocacy of Laws and
Public Policies 63
III. The Charge of Exclusivism toward Religious
Reasons 70
IV. Natural Reason, Secularity, and Religious
Conviction 76
V. Religious Reasons, Political Decision, and
Toleration 86
IV. Privatization versus Activism: The Place of Religious
Considerations in Public Political Discourse 90

4. Democratic Tolerance and Religious Obligation
in a Globalized World 105
I. The Nature of Tolerance 106
II. Is Tolerance a Virtue? 108
III. Toleration and Forgiveness 113
IV. The Normative Standards for Democratic
Toleration 115
V. Religion in the Workplace as a Test Case for a Theory
of Toleration 123
VI. Cosmopolitanism as a Framework for Tolerance 129
VII. Civic Virtue and Democratic Participation 134
VIII. International Implications of the Framework 148

Conclusion 151

Notes 157
Index 175

PREFACE AND ACKNOWLEDGMENTS

The relation between church and state—between religious and governmental institutions—is perhaps of greater interest now than at any time in living memory. This applies also to a closely related topic that is also central in this book: the relation between ethics and religion and the role of both in guiding the political conduct of citizens in democratic societies. These topics are of concern not only in political theory but also in law, religion, the social sciences, and numerous other fields. One or another aspect of the topics arises in the popular media, in myriad periodicals, and in classrooms, churches, legislative chambers, and elsewhere.

I have written much on the separation of church and state and on the ethics of citizenship as it applies to individuals. But years of discussing these topics with the general public as well as with colleagues and students have convinced me that there is a need for a short, highly readable book that both extends and refines the ideas developed in my earlier work. My aim here is to bring forward an overall perspective on the intersection of ethics, religion, and politics and to do so in a way that will interest readers new to the topic but also reward those who have been reflecting on it for a long time.

This book is both strongly separationist regarding church and state and highly accommodationist regarding standards for the relation between governments and religious institutions.

Some readers might find it too accommodating; others might find it insufficiently so. But anyone interested in the topic is likely to find much to explore and much to debate. No strong position on the problems that this book addresses can be uncontroversial, but it is possible to bring greater clarity and more nuanced standards to the debate and to provide concepts, standards, and conceptual tools that can be fruitfully used by all who conscientiously consider the separation of church and state or the relation between religion and politics in the lives of citizens in pluralistic democracies.

The individual chapters are largely self-contained, and the notes accompanying them often indicate further reading. Chapter 1 in particular is both self-contained and concise; it provides background theory that strengthens the position of the book as a whole. This chapter is mainly about ethics in relation to theology and religion, and it paves the way for political philosophy without making explicit points in that field. Chapter 1 is not required for comprehension of what follows, but the position of the book is cumulatively set out, and I hope that readers who concentrate on a subset of the chapters will at least selectively consider the others. Chapter 1 is important for the full-scale defense of the overall view; but it may be of greatest interest only to philosophically or theologically oriented readers, and the elements it contains that are needed for direct support of other chapters are usually referred at the relevant points.

I regret that the need for brevity and accessibility has at times forced me to omit both arguments and references, but my hope is that readers who miss those will be able to find many through the notes citing my own work on the topic and that of other authors (though regrettably far fewer than I know of) who have contributed to it. Some of the notes also indicate substantive issues that cannot be pursued in the text. In places, I discuss the contrasting views of other writers in the field, but to do full justice to even those few would require a great deal of space. I hope, however, that it will be clear to readers who know the literature that I have tried to take account of far more related writings than I discuss or even refer to and that I appreciate the plausibility of views different from my own.

Acknowledgments

For helpful discussion or the issues and, in many cases, comments on my work or writings from which I have benefited, I want to thank John Broome, Roger Crisp, Mario De Caro, Christopher Eberle, Rainer Forst, Richard Garnett, Jon Garthoff, Kent Greenawalt, James Gustafson, William Hasker, Brad Hooker, Mark Jensen, Stephen Kalish, Simo Knuuttila, Andrew Koppelman, Cristina Lafont, Craig Lawson, George Letsas, Daniel McKaughan, Paolo Monti, Thomas Nagel, Michael Perry, Michael Quante, the late Philip L. Quinn, Thomas Schmidt, Ludwig Siep, Andreas Speer, John Tasioulas, Paul Weithman, Nicholas Wolterstorff, Laurie Zoloth, and, especially, Jack Sammons. Numerous other colleagues and many students have also contributed to my thinking on the topic, particularly in seminars I have given at Northwestern and at Notre Dame (where comments by Michael Deem, Daniel Immerman, Jeremy Neill, Bryan Pilkington, and Caleb Perl were helpful at a late stage).

Lecture series I have presented at Kings College London, Santa Clara University, the University of Cologne, the University of Muenster, Northwestern University (as the Brady Lectures), and Wake Forest University (as the Thomas J. Lynch Lectures), have been particularly helpful, as have numerous paper presentations at conferences and in many colleges and universities. The benefits of these discussions and the many respondents from whom I have learned are too numerous to list. I have also benefited over the years from a number of comments by anonymous referees. I thank all of these people and only hope that this book reflects as much as it should of what I learned on those occasions.

My hearty thanks to Peter Ohlin for editorial support and advice, to Philip Wolny for great help in production, and to Lucy Randall for facilitating much of the work in planning for publication of the book.

Previous work from which I have selectively drawn includes mainly the following: *Religion in the Public Square* (Rowman and Littlefield, 1997, written jointly with Nicholas Wolterstorff), *Religious Commitment and Secular Reason* (Cambridge University Press, 2000), *The Good in the Right: A Theory of Intuition and Intrinsic Value* (Princeton University Press, 2004), and numerous papers published in journals, law reviews, and edited volumes. The theory of *The Good in the Right*, which sets out a comprehensive ethical view, supports the overall position of the book. It is not presupposed as an essential basis, but it does provide plausible elements that people with many different ethical orientations can accept. Other connections with my previous work are indicated in the notes.

DEMOCRATIC AUTHORITY

AND

THE SEPARATION OF CHURCH AND STATE

INTRODUCTION

The contemporary world is seeing two contrasting trends. One is toward a secular outlook on life. The other is toward religious fundamentalism. Democratic states tend to be highly secular, and many are becoming more so even as, in some of them, fundamentalist religious groups are growing. Tensions are inevitable and mounting, but must there also be violent clashes? Is there a political philosophy that can sustain a democratic tolerance both by and of religious citizens? Are there plausible, teachable principles on which both religious and secular citizens can participate cooperatively in public life? A democratic state should protect the liberty of its citizens and, accordingly, should accommodate both religious liberty and cultural diversity in religion and in other realms of life. Religious citizens, however, commonly see a secular state as unfriendly toward religion. A major aim of this book is to articulate a framework of principles that enables secular governments to provide for the liberty of all in a way that observes a reasonable separation of church—meaning religious institutions—and state and minimizes alienation of religious citizens.

My method in developing this framework in a new way is to begin with the relation between religion and ethics. This relation is crucial for political philosophy but insufficiently accounted for by philosophers, theologians, and political theorists. If the ethical standards that should govern human life depend on religion, it is easy to see why religious citizens might think that the morality sanctioned by their faith should structure their government. If, by contrast, religion has no moral authority, it is easy to see why secular citizens should think that, guided by universal moral rights, the state may limit religious practices.

The position I construct in Chapter 1 shows how, as a quest for sound moral standards, ethics can be independent of religion—evidentially autonomous in a way that makes moral knowledge possible for secular citizens—without presupposing that religion and theology have no moral authority of their own. That ethics does not in this way depend on religion is often denied by religious people; that religion and theology have moral authority is often denied by secular thinkers. In arguing against both of these negative views I draw on extensive work in ethical theory and seek to enhance mutual understanding among their proponents.

On the basis of that previous work, I briefly introduce a new version of divine command theory in ethics, a theory which (though I do not myself hold it) I believe is both plausible and consonant with piety. This theory leaves room for moral knowledge that is independent of religion, but it also provides a view of moral obligation on which our obligations are consonant with many kinds of theistic commitments. Chapter 1 is not, however, centered on divine command ethics; its main purpose is to set out a position in ethics that supports the kind of separation of church and state, and the associated ethics of citizenship, defended in the book as a whole. The divine command theory is set out mainly to show how, within a traditional theistic framework, religious people can accept ethical principles of the kind essential for guiding both democratic governments and political conduct by individuals. (The details of this theory—as with many points in Chapter 1—are not often presupposed in later chapters except where explicitly noted.)

Given what is established in Chapter 1, it is clear why a democratic society that protects religious liberty might wish to maintain a separation of church and state. A major support for this separation is the idea that citizens should not be subject to coercion, whether through laws or through public policies, unless it is justified by reasons that can be understood and appreciated by rational, adequately informed adults independently of their religious position. Chapter 2 portrays a kind of church-state separation that accommodates both religious and secular citizens. A well-designed separation enables government to deal with important issues in contemporary life. One such issue is the treatment of evolutionary biology in the science curriculum of public schools. A related problem is the legitimacy of vouchers to pay for private school education. Still another issue is governmental support of "faith-based initiatives," such as church-affiliated, governmentally supported shelters for the homeless. The theory of church-state separation presented in this chapter bears on all of these problems and (to use the terminology of the legal literature) takes account of both establishment issues concerning religion and free exercise issues.

The optimal balance between secularity in the state—which in practice implies a kind of governmental neutrality toward religion—and protection of religious liberty requires at least two kinds of principles: *institutional principles*, such as those appropriate to constitutions and to legislation, and *individual principles* articulating standards of civic virtue that apply to individual conduct. Chapter 2 concerns mainly the former, Chapter 3 mainly the latter. My previous work has stressed, as necessary for justified support of coercive laws and public policies, "adequate secular reason"—a kind of religiously neutral reason—and in earlier work I have explicated both adequacy and secularity—though not in all the aspects discussed here. John Rawls has used the different, though overlapping, terminology of "public reason," and both views (among others addressing the same problem) have been widely examined.

Chapter 3 connects the idea of secular reason with what, historically—particularly from Thomas Aquinas on—has been called "natural reason." Natural reason (though perhaps not "public reason") is a basic human endowment manifested in everyday reasoning, and it is prominently recognized (though usually under different names), and indeed central, in some major religions. Part of my task is to show how the kind of governmental neutrality I defend is consonant with natural reason—roughly, reason as a natural endowment of normal adult human beings—even if the latter is taken, as it has been by philosophical theologians since medieval times, to provide sufficient grounds for accepting theism, say as the only good explanation of why there is a world at all, or as the best explanation of the natural order, or as evidenced by other matters of ordinary fact.

A theistically oriented conception of natural reason poses a challenge to liberal political theory that has not been generally noticed. Suppose we make the plausible assumption that democracies may not properly assume that natural reason, which is shared by us all and does not rely on religious premises, cannot establish theism. Democracies would then seem to lack an adequate basis for a truly robust separation of church and state, one that rules out establishing even the generic "civil religion" historically present in the United States, though perhaps now declining in most quarters. How can a democracy completely separate church and state if the proper use of human reason as shared by us all regardless of religious commitment leads to a theistic outlook? Without good grounds for a robust separation of church and state, democratic theory cannot justify the far-reaching governmental neutrality toward religion endorsed by liberal political theory. Chapter 3 is partly devoted to addressing this challenge to liberal political theory.

The first three chapters, then, clarify how an adequate conception of the proper relation between religion and politics is needed not just for political philosophy but also as an element in the constitutional development of evolving nations and as a contribution to peaceful coexistence in and among nations. But many questions remain concerning the kinds and limits of tolerance that are appropriate within the theory of religion and politics which the book provides. The final chapter proposes standards of tolerance that are supported by the theory and are partly constitutive of civic virtue. These standards will be shown to be harmonious both with major, widely shared ethical views and with the reciprocity appropriate to the principles I propose in the ethics of citizenship.

The final chapter also addresses the not uncommon cases (such as stem cell research and capital punishment) in which we may find ourselves in disagreement with people we consider equally rational and equally informed on the issue in question. The principles of tolerance proposed for these cases will be framed on the basis of an account of rational disagreement I have developed elsewhere.[1] In the light of my theory of religion and politics and my related account of tolerance, this chapter will also address such global issues as religion in the workplace, the rights of women, and the tension between nationalism and cosmopolitanism.

Overall, the book will advance the theory of liberal democracy, clarify the relation between religion and ethics, provide distinctive principles governing religion in politics, and outline a theory of toleration. It frames institutional principles for the guidance of governmental policy toward religious institutions; it articulates citizenship standards for political conduct by individuals; it examines the case for affirming these two kinds of standards on the basis of what, historically, has been called natural reason; and it defends an account of toleration that enhances the practical application of the overall ethical framework.

CHAPTER 1

THE AUTONOMY OF ETHICS AND THE MORAL AUTHORITY OF RELIGION

Historically, religion and ethics are inextricably intertwined. But the historically inseparable may be logically independent. Ethics does not evidentially depend on religion or theology, and at least a great deal of religion and theology does not evidentially depend on ethics; but any society in which both religion and ethics are major cultural elements will function best if, in addition to a widespread recognition of this independence, there is fruitful interaction between the two. I have in mind not only interactions between ethical and religious elements in the thinking of those committed to both. I am also referring to interactions between religious citizens and non-religious citizens in matters on which religion and ethics bear. These interactions include, of course, at least the majority of issues that properly concern citizens in modern pluralistic democracies.

The focus of this book is not on mere democracies—societies that are simply governed by democratic procedures independently of moral constraints of the kind a sound constitution should affirm—or even forms of government ethically superior to those but only barely meeting the standard implicit in the notion of government of, by, and for the people. The focus is liberal democracies. These are democracies in which a commitment to preservation of a kind of maximal liberty is a basic structural element. To be sure, without basic political liberty, the votes of citizens do not suffice to render a government they elect "by" the people at all. But a liberal democracy seeks to preserve what, in rough terms, we might call the highest level of liberty all can have without interfering with the liberty of others. More will be said about how this standard may be achieved, especially in relation to religious liberty.

A second major element in liberal democracy is a strong commitment to preserving a kind of basic political equality. This kind of equality entails a one-person one-vote standard and might have manifestations as simple as facilitating voter registration and transportation to polls, and as complex as establishing restrictions on institutional and financial influences in politics.[1] If, as an individual citizen, I vote once on a proposition on the ballot or on candidates for office, I should not be permitted to cast further votes by purchasing them from other citizens. Much more could be said about what makes a democracy liberal in the sense sketched, but for the most part I shall simply presuppose this sense and speak of democracy as such.

I also presuppose that democracy as a form of government is morally justifiable and properly constituted by a commitment to respect certain rights—above all, rights to liberty and to basic political equality, which I take to entail adhering to the standard of one person, one vote.[2] If we are to regard democracy as in principle morally well-grounded and on that basis to provide a theory of church-state separation, it is important to consider the relation between ethics and religion. If ethics and political philosophy—which is in part ethics writ large—are not in a certain way independent of religion, this will undermine the kind of separationist position that, on my view, is essential for sound democratic government. I mean, of course, a normatively sound government: one that meets the appropriate standards, in ethics and political philosophy, for good democratic governance. Similarly, a sound democracy is *structured* so that its government meets such standards. What these standards are is a major topic in itself, and this book contributes to the topic only in one important area: church-state relations and associated relations between religion and politics in the conduct of individual citizens.

I. The Autonomy of Ethics

I begin, then, by considering what, in general, constitutes the *epistemic*—roughly, evidential—autonomy of a domain of apparent knowledge, such as ethics. I take the epistemic autonomy of a domain to be its independence of other domains of knowledge, in this limited sense: knowledge in the autonomous domain does not necessarily depend on knowledge, or on justification for beliefs, in some other domain. Thus, if knowledge of a moral truth, say that lying is (with some exceptions) wrong, is unqualifiedly autonomous, then this knowledge is possible other than by virtue of knowing something in a different domain.[3] We would not need premises, for instance, about the long-term negative effects of lying on human communication.

Moral Knowledge and "Descriptive" Fact

Could ethics be epistemically independent in this strong sense? How could we know that lying is wrong apart from knowing such non-moral facts as that it leads to mistrust, undermines cooperation, and arouses anger? Call the latter kind of non-ethical knowledge *descriptive*—roughly, knowledge of what *is*—to mark a contrast with ethical knowledge, which is roughly knowledge of what *ought* to be, or is (in itself) *good* or *bad*. (Descriptive knowledge of this kind is also natural knowledge, a notion to be discussed in detail in chapter 3). Clearly, some moral knowledge depends in part on perceptual knowledge, such as knowledge based on seeing or hearing, or at least on having evidential grounds for such knowledge, as where we see a mugging and thereby know a wrong was done. This certainly holds (as will shortly be illustrated) for some cases.

There is, however, a difference between the way in which *general* moral knowledge depends on descriptive knowledge and the way moral knowledge of particular actions so depends. Take general moral knowledge first. We should grant that one cannot know that lying is wrong without having the concepts of, for instance, believing, speaking, falsifying, and misleading. This illustrates a *conceptual* dependence of ethics on non-moral notions. It is no surprise that knowledge requires having the concepts needed for understanding the proposition known. Conceptual dependence on non-moral notions is no threat to the epistemic autonomy of ethics. Compare moral knowledge of a single action. We cannot know that a particular action is wrong without knowing such things as that it is a mugging, a lie, a promise-breaking, or a neglect of easily relieved suffering. This illustrates a kind of perceptual dependence that *is* epistemic. Still, dependence on perception is a kind such moral knowledge shares with scientific knowledge. Neither kind of dependence shows that ethical knowledge depends on any religious view or theological idea.[4]

Independence of Religion versus Independence of God

My point, then, is not that ethics is epistemically autonomous in an absolute sense. Rather, it is autonomous *relative to* religion and even theology. This is not the claim that we could know moral truths if there *are* no theological or religious truths, above all, if there should be no God. The point is that knowledge of moral truths does not depend on *knowledge* of God or of religious truths (or on justification for religious or theological propositions). This view is not anti-religious and indeed has been held by theists at least since St. Thomas Aquinas. Indeed, one might well think that God would want us to be able to have moral knowledge on a non-religious basis. Having such a basis enables us to know, and even to realize, moral standards quite apart from our having religious knowledge.

One might now wonder whether there is any realm of knowledge that, evidentially, *is* absolutely independent. Perhaps elementary logical knowledge, say that no proposition is both true and false, is entirely autonomous. Whether it is or not, its appearing to have this lofty status is part of what fuels skepticism: no other cognitive domain (roughly, a domain of belief and apparent knowledge) meets this standard. Why, then, should we accept anything less cogent? I do not find this skeptical challenge compelling, and in this book I largely set philosophical skepticism aside. Even if we suppose that perception is second best in providing knowledge, second best need by no means be second rate. Indeed, the price of epistemic invulnerability is a certain modesty of content. Logic is utterly abstract and tells us nothing about what specific propositions about our world are true or false.

II. Moral Knowledge: General and Particular

The history of moral thought contains many attempts to show that—in my terms—ethics is a domain in which there are important truths that are naturally, and hence secularly, knowable. On my theory of moral knowledge, human reason—in the form of intuitive thinking—can reveal moral truths. My point of departure is an extension and rational reconstruction of the intuitionist position of W. D. Ross, a position often credited with representing reflective common sense.[5] In providing this comprehensive intuitive framework, I represent ethics as a domain in which we can have a priori moral knowledge and a priori justification—roughly, knowledge and justification that come through intuition or reflection rather than social-scientific inquiry or other kinds of empirical inquiry. The knowledge and justification are not, however, indefeasible: far from licensing absolutism or

dogmatic certitude, this view allows that we can be fully justified in believing something but still mistaken. Even when we
are fully justified in believing something or indeed know it,
we may have no right to *claim* we do.

What might be candidates for moral knowledge of this
intuitive kind? Consider some of the "prima facie duties"
described by Ross—obligations that are defeasible but prevail as our overall obligation if there is no equally weighty
opposing set of duties. There are duties (moral obligations)
not to injure others, not to lie or break promises, and, positively, to do beneficent deeds. These are real obligations
intrinsic to the human condition: given our status as sentient rational beings with the kind of agency that makes
social interaction possible, there is necessarily a *moral reason*
to fulfill these obligations strong enough so that, in the
absence of any conflicting obligation, we ought—in an overall sense—to act accordingly. We may have promises to keep
that preclude our doing all we would like to for a friend in
need, but this shows that the obligation of beneficence is
overridden, not that it has no moral force in the context.

It must be granted, however, that the knowledge that we
ought, prima facie, not to injure, lie, and so forth, is quite
modest. For we can know that we have a prima facie obligation, hence a moral reason, to do something without knowing
that we should in the end actually *do* it. A reason to vote
against a school bond as benefiting too few citizens might be
outweighed by a reason to help the children of the needy, for
whom the bond provides nutritious lunches; but even
knowing that the latter is preferable might leave us uncertain
whether a third, competing measure is what we ought finally
to support. If our knowledge of certain moral principles is
broadly a priori, then, it is also limited. The price of such intuitive knowledge is (as our examples show) a certain modesty of practical content. To be sure, such modest moral
content—say, that we should keep our promises—is not as

abstract as formal logic. But it is highly general. Yet it is *singular* moral judgments, such as that *I* should keep my promise to help you tomorrow, that must guide our moral lives.

May we, however—or may some of us—bring religious or theological commitments or insights to bear in determining singular moral judgments? Might such insights or commitments inform our practical ethics? This is a major question I will address shortly.

III. Religion, Theology, and Ethics

Let us first ask: If ethics is autonomous relative to religion, should we affirm the converse? Is religion autonomous relative to ethics? Some would argue that religion arose in the first place to support ethics—or at least the ethos of its surrounding culture.[6] Suppose religion did arise because of its support of ethics (or enough of ethics to conduce to human survival). One might be tempted to conclude that religion cannot be evidentially independent of ethics. This would not follow. As to the supposition, I won't pursue historical or sociological questions about the origins or social function of religion. My interest is in epistemic autonomy: Could one have *evidence* of a non-ethical kind supporting a religion?

Natural Theology and the Concept of Goodness

Unless we distinguish religion from theology, this question is unmanageable. There are simply too many religions of too many kinds. But we can sensibly ask whether natural theology—by which I mean (roughly) reflection on theological matters using natural reason independently of religion or revealed theology—can be supported without ethical premises. The most plausible arguments for God's existence do not depend on moral premises; they proceed to theological conclusions from what might be called natural facts, such as those evident to ordinary perception or discernment of a kind possible for all normal human beings.[7] A famous example of such a putative fact is that nature exhibits a kind of design. Theism can be argued for without moral premises. Moral premises, however, do not exhaust value premises. If we make the common assumption that God is omnibenevolent—essentially perfectly good—and that goodness is central to the very concept of God, then evidence for God's existence must in some way take account of this assumption if it is to support a theism that justifies an ethic for human life. That would require evidence that embodies at least a *concept* of goodness. That in turn would apparently require that adequate evidence for the existence of God must make some presuppositions about what constitutes the good. Natural theology, then, might proceed independently of specifically moral presuppositions, but not without presuppositions about the good.

Nothing said here implies that non-theistic religions are unimportant or that a theistic religion is of interest in this book only if it posits a deity who is all-knowing, all-powerful, and perfectly good. But it is theistic religious of this latter kind—especially Christianity, Judaism, and Islam—that raise the most pressing contemporary problems concerning the separation of church and state and of religion and politics. Such monotheistic religions are thus my central concern.

The Moral Authority of Religion

Suppose then, that natural theology does depend on some non-theological notion of the good. This conclusion is compatible with the view that a plausible case from natural theology for the existence of a perfectly good God can be made without presupposing moral propositions. Suppose that view is sound. What might we conclude about the moral authority of theology or indeed of religion: about whether claims based on theological or religious views can have some evidential weight independently of secular moral knowledge? Should we conclude that, since a concept of goodness must be presupposed by a sound natural theology, neither natural theology nor a religion that is built on it can have moral authority? I think not.

Suppose there is evidence from natural theology for the existence of God as usually conceived in Western religions: minimally, as all-knowing, all-powerful, and perfectly good. And suppose that there are moral truths—as there must be if I am right in thinking we know some. Then, from God's omniscience—God's knowing *all* (knowable) truths—we may infer two conclusions of considerable importance for understanding the issues of church-state separation and of the ethics of bringing religious considerations into political decision. The first conclusion is that God knows all moral truths; second, from God's goodness we may apparently conclude that God would wish us to act on those truths. How could a perfectly good being not wish us to act morally?

These conclusions are highly abstract. There is still the problem of getting from the view that there *are* general moral truths to clear formulations of them, and from those formulations to singular moral judgments—the kind that, like my judgment that I ought not to vote to illegalize wearing Islamic headscarves, guide everyday life. But suppose there is a sound natural theology. Indeed, even if there is not, suppose there is a God and that some religions and some scriptures provide indications of what God would have us do. To fix ideas, consider the Bible (this is not to deny that other scriptural texts might also serve as an example).

Might good interpretations of Biblical ethical standards have some moral authority at least *for* those who have a rational commitment to their authenticity as in some way inspired by God? If so, this authority would apparently still be only that of prima facie principles. This would not, however, differentiate them from intuitive moral principles knowable by natural reason. Indeed the Biblical prohibitions of killing and lying are equivalent to intuitive moral principles which have secular formulations and admit of exceptions such as self-defense in the same way. Nor does anything said here imply that there need be any conflicts between the best moral judgments we can make on a secular basis and the best we can draw from reflection on the ethical content of our scripture—modified, presumably, by connecting it with one's religious tradition and other elements bearing on its interpretation.

There is, moreover, a kind of ethical safety net available from natural theology as I have sketched it. Given the presupposition that God is essentially good, it is plausible to maintain that any apparent command to do what is clearly on balance wrong—such as genocidal killing, or torturing children for pleasure—cannot come from God. Let me put the point more generally. Suppose that (as I hold) we may rationally claim a priori knowledge (knowledge based on a kind of reflection alone) of certain moral principles and, on the basis of them together with ordinary facts, can know certain singular, action-guiding moral propositions. Then, by and large, we may attribute greater credibility to moral judgments in this commonsensical range than to conflicting ones made by scripture or—especially—by its interpreters, such as authoritarian clergy who seek to influence the conduct of citizens. What is supported by reason and everyday facts may be reasonably viewed (even by religious people) as having prima facie (though not absolute) epistemic priority over moral claims based *only* on religious grounds, especially if these grounds depend on fallible interpretations of scriptures or other religious sources.[8]

The Plural Sources of Moral Knowledge

This point is quite consistent with my suggestion that a theology or indeed a particular religion may, adequately interpreted, have some degree of moral authority. Moreover, I have not meant to suggest that whatever moral authority it has must come from its specifically theological or religious side. Nothing whatever stops theologians or religious people from having (as they often do) practical wisdom or from drawing moral inspiration from multiple sources that go beyond, and may indeed help in interpreting, their scriptures.

Indeed, insofar as ethics is autonomous because it contains principles accessible to natural reason, we should expect that moral knowledge *not* based on, say, scripture or some other religious element should arise for many religious people in ways that do not depend on their religion. In the light of these points, it is evident that theologians and religious people can sometimes have a moral authority that reflects a combination of sources. This can enhance their authority or—depending on the sources—adulterate it. But that there can be some degree of prima facie moral authority on the part of some religious people as such seems undeniable.

It will be clarifying to distinguish three kinds of moral authority, only one of which is of major concern here. First, there is *psychological authority* in moral matters—a kind of influence over one or more persons. Typically, this authority is exercised by one person over one or more others by the former's appealing to knowing the relevant subject-matter in a way superior to their way of knowing it. Second, there is *cultural-historical authority* in moral matters—which religions, conceived sociologically, can have over large-scale events, such as social practices and wars. This, like psychological authority, is a kind of influence. Third, there is *normative authority* in moral matters—roughly the capacity to supply reasons for belief or for action or both. This has been my main concern, and I have suggested how theology or religion may, in certain cases, have a measure of normative authority on questions of right and wrong.

Nothing said here implies that the moral authority of theology or religion is *basic,* in the way the evidential authority of perception seems to be. For instance, the relevant theological premises and the other elements that might lead to knowing a divine moral command would not be evidentially basic, though they also need not be moral or dependent on making prior moral judgments. Still, the normative strength of an authority is not directly proportional to how close it is to being basic. Testimony is a less basic source of knowledge than perception. But in some matters, some people's testimony is a more reliable source than other people's perceptions.

IV. Theoethical Equilibrium: The Integration of Religion and Ethics

Once we see that theology and religion can have moral authority of the special kind I have outlined, we may take a special interest in how to integrate whatever ethical insight can be gained from them with moral knowledge, or apparent moral knowledge, grounded in secular reason. I have already suggested an approach to this question. Let me now develop it.

Reflective Equilibrium in Ethical Matters

For some religious people, it will be not unnatural to try to maintain or reach reflective equilibrium among their beliefs and attitudes grounded in what they take to be religious sources of obligation. In general terms, reflective equilibrium is a condition of balance among our general principles, concrete cases that they apply to, and related beliefs and attitudes that we may hold.[9] For instance, Biblically oriented religious people might try to square their personal beliefs about their general obligations of self-development and family support—beliefs that can easily be self-serving—with such beneficence as is portrayed in the story of the Good Samaritan and in other religious texts calling for assistance to the poor.

In some instances, there is also a need for religious people to find a reflective equilibrium among the obligations that emerge for them in this religiously based equilibrium *and*, on the other side, beliefs and attitudes they hold or find plausible which they take to be grounded in secular sources, such as some involving stem cell research or child labor. These, they may think, are not clearly treated by scripture or other authoritative sources. Roughly, this effort to find reflective equilibrium of a comprehensive ethical kind is a search for a cognitive balance in which the elements in question—chiefly one's beliefs, attitudes, and desires—are mutually consistent and, so far as possible, mutually supportive. If moral reflection convinces me of certain moral principles and these seem central in my scriptures and appropriate to approval by God as perfectly good, I am likely to be and to feel in equilibrium. If, on the other hand, my scriptures seem to support both capital punishment and the sanctity of all human lives, I will be in disequilibrium.

The more rational we are, and the more complicated the moral issues we face, the wider the equilibrium we are likely to seek. The elements we seek to interconnect in reflective equilibrium may reasonably extend, though they need not, to theology, ethical theory, and scientific considerations.[10] Thus, preferring to use some of one's earnings to support church renovations over a new ballpark might fit best with one's religious commitments. By contrast, the thought of supporting a candidate who favors most of one's sociopolitical policies but is also stingy regarding educational funding may produce an ambivalence that precludes reaching reflective equilibrium in one's secular ethical thinking and may prevent making a contribution. In developing a stance as an active voting citizen, I should take account of both my religious commitments and my secular ethical views, as well as my scientific outlook. If I succeed in getting all these elements in a balance that facilitates moral and other practical decisions, I will have a kind of rationale for much of my conduct and can better explain myself to others, including people with different religious views.

Integrating Religious and Secular Beliefs and Attitudes

I call this kind of reflective balance between religiously and secularly based moral beliefs and attitudes *theoethical equilibrium*. It is not unreasonable to construe the search for it as a prima facie obligation of at least those religious people who want to have as well-developed and reasonable a moral outlook as possible, or who want to have as good a case as they can for persuading others outside their faith to join them in a view or activity. Achieving such persuasion often depends on finding common secular ground for the moral position in question. But what reason is there to think that theoethical equilibrium is generally achievable for religious people?

To see this, assume a broadly Western theism, on which God is all-knowing, all-powerful, and perfectly good. Might we not—given this set of divine attributes and abstracting from any particular theology—expect God to structure us free rational beings *and* the world of our experience so that there is a (humanly accessible) secular path—roughly, a path ascertainable by natural reason—to discovering moral truths, at least those far-reaching truths needed for the kind of civilized life we can assume God would wish us to live? Let me develop this idea.

A conscientious search for theoethical equilibrium need not presuppose that either secular or religious ethical standards have unqualified priority over the other. The search may result in changes in one's secular ethical views or one's religiously based ethical views or both. Even if I believe my religious position must take priority in any case of conflict, I might still be strongly motivated to avoid irreconcilable conflict. Qualifying my views on either side as a result of interaction with the other need not imply giving the latter priority. A maple and copper beech standing side by side are two very different trees, but both can be nourished by the ground they share, and each can enhance the growth and strength of the other with no change in their essential characteristics.

The Religious Ambiguity of the World

It might be denied that there is any secular path to moral truths, and if one imagines that (perhaps because of sin) human reason is corrupted, this may seem to be our fate. But even countenancing original sin does not necessitate taking this view in interpreting the Bible, and I am in any case trying to theorize in an ecumenical way independent of any particular theology. One plausible assumption acceptable to people in various theistic religions is that God has created a religiously ambiguous world, a world admitting both theistic and non-theistic understandings—the latter because evil is so prominent as to tempt even many theists to conclude that this sorry world cannot be created by *God*. Why God might create a world with evils of the kind we find—the perennial "problem of evil"—is a major issue on which much has been written.[11] What should be said here is that many theologians and philosophers consider the importance of human freedom to be so great that God would permit moral evil as an unavoidable consequence of allowing genuine freedom. On this view, it is not possible even for God to create us genuinely free *and* prevent evil.

Whatever one's view on the problem of evil, one can see that it is one thing for God to test us and provide challenging conditions for our freely choosing to become children of God (a prominent theistic rationale for the existence of great evils); it would be quite another thing for God to make it virtually impossible for those who do not so choose, even to be moral in non-theological matters.[12] At least for those who conscientiously try to find reason to believe in God and cannot, it would seem unconsonant with divine goodness to add to their loss in failing to recognize their beneficent creator by making it impossible for them even to discover how they should behave in daily life.

Thus, in addition to the intuitive plausibility of affirming non-religiously based knowledge of some moral principles (such as those expressing the prima facie obligations cited above), there is some theological reason to think that God would create us able to know these without depending on theology. God would not give us freedom even to reject our creator and deny us the possibility of at least being moral in secular conduct.

Divinity and Secularity

If the freedom preserved by the religious ambiguity of the world is valuable enough to provide a possible explanation of God's permitting that ambiguity, should we not, then, expect God to provide for access to rational standards, discoverable by secular inquiry, for the proper exercise of that freedom, as opposed to its abuse or waste in immoral, wrongheaded, or ignorant behavior? If God cares enough about us not to compel us toward theism, but instead allows our free choice or rejection of it, would it not seem that God would equip us with standards for the use of our freedom in the ways appropriate to God's creatures? Even if one attributes much of our misfortune to our own sin, one might reasonably expect that God would not allow us to be deprived of a way to know the minimum standards required to understand our own wrongdoing and to use our freedom to rectify it.

Some theologies would not receive this argument sympathetically. But there are certainly plausible theological assumptions on which the argument can be strengthened. Moreover, the conclusion that there are moral standards knowable through natural reason is one to which many theological traditions—certainly the natural law tradition deriving from Aquinas—are favorable.[13] This view is in any case of sufficient independent plausibility to be assumed in the qualified form needed here.

V. Divine Command Ethics and Secular Morality

For some people, the perspective on ethics so far presented gets the cart before the horse. Isn't God the source of moral standards, and so, shouldn't theology and religion be our primary basis for those standards? How can the devout accept theoethical equilibrium as even making sense for them, much less as worth seeking? They can if they can countenance the possibility that there may be at least two ways to achieve moral knowledge: one religious and the other secular.

Two Routes to Moral Knowledge

Suppose one holds a divine command ethics, one that makes God's commands central in determining our basic moral obligations. Must one then not give up the autonomy of ethics? If, for instance, our obligations simply *are* to do what God commands, how could ethics not depend on theology? Knowing right and wrong would seem to require knowing divine will. Notice, however, that the implied identity of the *property* of obligatoriness with divine commandedness does not imply that the *concept* of the obligatory or other moral concepts are theological. The divine command view I am sketching is not, for instance, that 'obligatory' *means* 'commanded by God'— that would not be plausible. It would imply (among other implausible consequences) that a person could not even learn moral vocabulary without acquiring religious concepts at the same time.

An implication of this conceptual difference between the obligatory and the divinely commanded is this. Although an obligatory type of *act* could not fail to be divinely commanded, at least implicitly, one could still *know* that a type of act is obligatory without *knowing* that it is divinely commanded. Identifying moral with theological properties does not automatically foreclose the number or variety of cognitive handles by which we can grasp moral properties. An analogy will clearly illustrate this. Just as one can know one is reading the author of *King Lear* without knowing one is reading the author of *The Winter's Tale* (another Shakespearean play, which readers of *Lear* need never have heard of), and just as one can know one is drawing a circle without knowing one is drawing the kind of plane figure whose circumference is its diameter times pi, one can know that an act is obligatory without knowing that it is divinely commanded.[14] We can conceive Shakespeare by two different descriptions he happened to satisfy, and we can characterize circles by two different properties they must have. Similarly, what we ought to do may be conceived in theological language or in secular moral terms. We might know divine will under a description drawn from the vocabulary of natural reason.

Divine Command Theory and Practical Ethics

In the light of the overall perspective so far sketched, it is not unreasonable to suppose that God would wish us to have many ways to discover our obligations. There are various reasons for this supposition. The existence of many non-theological ways of ascertaining our obligations might enhance the probability of right conduct for non-believers. They would have more ways of discovering it, including, of course, a non-religious way. Even for religious believers, a diversity of routes to moral knowledge might at least reinforce moral conduct. They are more likely to know what they ought to do; and different routes to this knowledge may involve different and often complementary incentives. I am more likely to give generously to charities if I see my obligation as *both* good citizenship and a religious duty.

Diversity of routes to moral knowledge might also add to believers' motivation and understanding regarding conduct even if they did not discover any obligations they were otherwise unaware of. It might also help them to determine what actions morality requires in cases where, as is not uncommon, this is not clear from their understanding of their religious commitments. These commitments may conflict with one another; they may also be insufficiently specific. Both points are illustrated by the obligations to honor one's parents and to help the poor—two obligations relevant to the kind of socio-political thinking important for this book. Moreover, for anyone concerned with explaining and justifying moral conduct, it is often valuable—or even essential—to have more than one perspective from which to frame an explanatory or justificatory account.

In practice, then, those who hold a form of divine command theory like the one sketched—as a natural law theorist might—can take a point of view from which they can see moral issues in non-theological terms as well as in theological or religious terms. In principle, they can view these issues much as do those who consider moral properties independent of divine will.

Given the suggested conception of divine command ethics, we can integrate the divine command and secular perspectives in a way that facilitates communication and debate in moral matters between religious and non-religious people. Suppose first that we take the property of being obligatory to be the same property as that of being divinely commanded. The obligation not to kill *is* the commandedness of this; the obligation to keep promises *is* the commandness of that; and so forth. But why stop there? Why not take *both* properties (i.e., the property expressed by the theological phrase 'divinely commanded' and the property expressed by the non-theological phrase 'being obligatory') to be *grounded* in non-moral, natural properties belonging to the type of obligatory act in question?[15] If there is just one property (obligatoriness), it should have one kind of grounding, even if it is conceivable in two quite different ways.

Consider, for instance, acts of loyalty to one's family or religious community. There are two kinds of considerations through which we can know these acts to be obligatory. First, from a secular ethical point of view, we can know they are obligatory in virtue of knowledge of our relations to these others—involving, say, one's promises of giving them support. The existence of such promises and of other commitment-grounding relations is a matter of ordinary fact and knowable by natural reason. Second, from a religious point of view, we can know from, say, scripture or religious experience, that God commands these acts of loyalty. Moreover, presumably God commands them at least in part *for* the very range of reasons constituted by the natural facts—such as promises made—that render them obligatory (this leaves open that God might also have other, perhaps quite different reasons). The divine commandedness of an act, which on this view is the same property as its obligatoriness, is thus in a sense *embedded* in its non-moral grounds: it is obligatory (commanded) because promised, or because honest, or because life-saving, and so forth.[16] The act is divinely commanded on the same grounds in virtue of which it is obligatory. The grounds might include the dignity of human persons as rational, sentient beings.

The Euthyphro Problem

We can now see how a proponent of divine command ethics might respond to the famous Euthyphro problem, which, in one version, is the problem of whether what is obligatory is such because God commands it or whether, instead, God commands it because it is obligatory.[17] Assuming that obligatoriness is the property of commandedness, we may deny *both* that the obligatory must be regarded as such because God commands it, i.e., as *grounded* in divine command, *and* that God commands it because it is obligatory. The first claim is mistaken because acts are obligatory on the basis of certain natural properties, say being promised or being life-saving. The second is mistaken because God commands acts on the basis of the morally crucial properties that *ground* their rightness, not simply on the basis of their being right (or obligatory). God is seen, then, as having a *reason*—indeed an a priori one—for regarding certain deeds as command-worthy and hence, *given* God's having sufficient reason to issue commands, for commanding those deeds. In short, we might say (in rough terms) that God commands obligatory acts not *because* they are right, *nor* are they obligatory because divinely commanded; rather, God commands them because of *why* they are right.

This divine command theory is in one way strong, since an act's being morally obligatory is *identified* with the theological property of its being divinely commanded. But in another way the theory is moderate: it provides a necessary *basis* for such commands, in the light of which we can understand both their infallibility and their corresponding to certain kinds of natural properties. These everyday natural properties are the very same ones in terms of which moral concepts are commonly understood, through using natural reason, whether outside or inside theological contexts. Moreover, in the light of these everyday properties we can see, even without relying on theological considerations, the appropriateness of the commands.

The grounding of the moral properties in natural ones can be (as I think it is in such cases) a priori as well as necessary. For instance, that killing people in pursuit of "ethnic cleansing" is wrong is not something merely contingently true, or something that must be learned by studying its causal consequences or otherwise gathering supporting empirical information. We can see its truth on the basis of adequately understanding its content—the immoral horrors it describes.[18]

Does the Theory Limit God?

It may seem that the kind of divine command theory in question would limit God. This is not so; instead, the theory brings out a way to understand both divine knowledge and indeed divine authority. Just as it is in virtue of their natural properties that God (infallibly) sees certain kinds of acts to be obligatory, God sees certain kinds of things to be good in virtue of *their* natural properties. In both cases, the relation between the different kinds of properties, the ethical and the descriptive ones, seems to be a necessary one. But just as any necessary truths are in some sense part of God's intellectual nature—eternally fixed points, as it were, in the divine conception of reality— any necessary goods are in some sense part of God's volitional nature. The necessary truths are unchangeable elements in the divine cognitive structure; the necessary goods are part of the basis of divine preferences. Like the moral truths, the truths about goodness are *within* God, not *above* God. God may indeed be seen as the highest possible exemplar of goodness.

Religious believers, then, can without impiety take moral properties to bear a special relation to natural ones. By clearly thinking about what ethnic cleansing is, they can know that it is wrong because it is a bigoted killing of men, women, and children. They can know a priori both that it is wrong and why—it wrongness is consequential on its lethal bigoted treatment of persons. This kind of natural moral knowledge is compatible with the identity of moral properties and certain theological ones, with the omniscience of God, and with God's consequent unerring authority in moral matters. Obeying (or pleasing) God can still be seen as central in both motivational and normative grounding of religious commitments.

This divine command theory allows for God—and indeed for religiously inspired people—to introduce new or refined moral standards. God need not establish moral principles in the way God establishes contingent natural patterns, in order to be the central focus of concern in obeying moral principles; and there can be a multitude of ways of coming to know those principles even for those whose deepest reason for abiding by them is religious. In the domain of ethics, then, religious commitment to what might be called classical theism neither unduly narrows one's theoretical and normative choices nor necessarily leads to judgments or conduct whose rationality is suspect even on the most rigorously secular grounds.

The Plural Sources of Moral Motivation

So far, I have shown how a theistic commitment, even if it includes a version of divine command ethics and thereby posits moral knowledge on the basis of religious sources, can also permit recognition of the epistemic autonomy of ethics. Moral knowledge is possible independently of reliance on theological knowledge or on justification for theological propositions, and the same holds for justification for moral judgments. It should also be clear that religious commitment can be reconciled with a variety of normative ethical theories, such as Kantianism, intuitionism, and some versions of natural law theory. I now want to consider the *motivational* grounding of moral commitments on the part of individuals. This is indeed the kind of religious grounding of morality that laypeople most often have in mind in speaking of religiously based morality as something that is both desirable and a requirement for commitment to religion. How is religious grounding of conduct possible given the autonomy of ethics and, especially, for a person who affirms it?

The question here is in part causal and explanatory. It partly concerns what causally sustains, or what provides a broadly causal explanation of, the elements whose grounds are queried. We can ask, regarding particular attitudinal and behavioral elements in particular people, whether they are based on, for instance, a text, a theology (whether revealed or natural), clerical directives, religious tradition, or religious experience, including experiences of divine directives. Here grounding in a text or theology or tradition is understood as grounding in *fidelity* to it, *belief* in it, or the like. The grounding is psychologically mediated by cognitive and motivational elements, and it is these—mainly beliefs on the cognitive side and desires and intentions on the motivational side—that actually motivate the agent.

To begin with, it seems quite clear that one could hold a divine command theory and still be motivated by *both* religious and secular considerations in one's ethical conduct. Not only could both kinds be motivating with respect to different acts; both could cooperate in motivating the same actions, such as self-sacrificial deeds of service to the poor. Each consideration may be sufficiently strong to produce the action by itself; but, for some actions, the two together may be needed. This doubly motivated conduct might include not only our actions in personal relationships or in doing service for an institution, but also our public conduct as citizens working to determine our society's laws and public policies. Even where a single type of action is in question, for instance serving in a soup kitchen, there may be some contexts in which one set of motives, say the religious, might act alone; in other cases, secular motivation might operate alone; and, over time, the mixture of motivational elements in a person might change.

A different example should add clarity. Suppose I believe that God has commanded honoring my parents. I may also feel, on the basis of secular ethical standards, an obligation to honor them. Even on the supposition that the property of divine commandedness on the part of such conduct is the same property as its moral requiredness (under, say, duties of fidelity), the *concepts* by which we apprehend these properties are different. Hence the *desires* to fulfill the two normative demands can be different. For desires with different conceptual content differ even if their different contents—say *to do one's duty toward one's parents* (a "secular" desire) and *to fulfill God's will toward one's parents* (a religious desire)—represent the same property.

An important point illustrated here is that one's intellectual view of the normative basis of moral standards is logically, and—to some extent—causally, independent of one's motivation in acting on those standards. One can be motivated very differently in meeting two compatible standards—or even the same one pursued under different conceptions. Consider the famous Biblical line about action in the service of religion versus wealth; "You cannot serve God and mammon." True enough, since the quests are incompatible; but you can serve God and morality. The quests are complementary.

Ethical Autonomy versus Ethical Isolation

I have been stressing both the possible identity of moral obligation with a theological property such as commandedness and the integration between religious and moral motivation. Do these kinds of far-reaching kinds of integration between religion and theology and, on the other hand, ethics imply that the autonomy of ethics is at least largely illusory? They do not. Nothing said here implies that the basic moral standards are religiously grounded in a normative sense; and both the knowability and the motivational power that are possible for them through theological or religious pathways are compatible with the autonomy of ethics.

To be sure, we may get a different impression if we consider a *non*-basic moral standard, say a religiously based principle requiring one to open one's church (in the broad sense of a religious institution) to all who want to join. This standard might be grounded in making a sacred promise, within one's church, to do so. Nonetheless, its normative force ultimately depends (for reasons already indicated) at least in part on something non-religious: the obligation-making character of promising. That relation is a necessary one that may be considered intrinsic to the divine nature.

How does this view apply if I am a religious believer who takes moral standards to be valid if and only if they are equivalent to the rules of conduct God has laid down for us *in the Bible*? May I not still endorse some secularly developed moral standard? And may I not be properly motivated in my ethical conduct by a commitment to this moral standard or by other non-religious factors, such as empathy and compassion? After all, these non-religious standards and motives may—and perhaps in some cases must—lead me to the same actions as a religious moral commitment. Still, the actions need not be intrinsically religious. Consider service to the sick, which is possible for non-theists. May I not adopt these non-religious standards as major guides to moral conduct?

The answer is clearly positive. For as long as I regard a secular moral standard as requiring the same conduct as my religiously based standard (or conduct consistent with it), I can respect the secular standard without impiety. If I can respect it, I can also be motivated by it as well as by my religious standard. My motivation might be dual in every case, as with relieving suffering, which is both religiously commanded and simply beneficent or, in some instances, either religious or secular but not both. It might also be blended in some way, depending on the context.

Consider an analogy. We can listen to two voices expressing the same directive, sometimes even when they are simultaneous.

One may be that of scripture, the other that of moral intuition or philosophical ethics. It is possible to be moved or indeed inspired by both, even if one voice is more authoritative for us. It is also possible to heed one of them alone, particularly where we take it that the other voice would (or does) concur. There may be times when we do a thing solely from compassion unconnected with our religion, even though we know that we are religiously enjoined to do the sort of thing in question. At other times, when, for instance, I realize that my respected secular standard requires doing justice to a heinous offender, or overcoming a strong prejudice, I may be so angry that only with my religiously required conduct firmly in mind am I able to keep just retribution from degenerating into revenge. The cooperation between religious and secular motives, like the integration of religiously inspired and secular ethical standards, can be morally quite positive.

————

We have seen how even a strong religious commitment may be harmonized with the autonomy of ethics, understood as the view that basic moral truths and the basic truths about the non-morally good and bad can be known or justifiedly believed on a non-theological basis. This epistemological view does not entail the metaphysical thesis that the *existence* of moral obligations and of intrinsically good things does not depend on God. The reason for that is not only the possibility that moral agents might not have existed apart from divine action; it is also possible that God *creates* certain obligations by such acts as commands, which require obedience, and by grace, which demands gratitude.

What of the ontological view that many moral propositions could be *true* in a world without God? Many theologians and philosophers have denied that such a world is possible, and nothing said here entails that it is. Ethics may be epistemically autonomous even if it is not possible. Moreover, not only may religious commitment be compatible with ethical theories as different as, say, divine command ethics, Kantianism, and intuitionism; it may also be integrated with a number of normative views, provided they accord an appropriate place to the worth of persons and to certain basic freedoms. There is no good reason to think, then, that a person of strong religious commitment cannot be, in ethical matters, at least as well-grounded as people guided by the major secular ethical theories presently available.

Although I am not endorsing a divine command ethical theory, I consider the version outlined to be a good one for reflective theists who, on the one hand, see God as central in undergirding both our moral standards and our practical commitments and, on the other hand, cannot regard the basic moral truths as contingent (and cannot understand how necessary truths could be established by God's will, as opposed to willed by God as appropriate to govern us). God is still seen as an infallible authority in moral matters, and obeying (or pleasing) God can still be central in both motivational and normative grounding of religious commitments. God need not establish moral principles in the way God establishes contingent natural patterns, in order to be the central focus of concern in obeying them; and there can be a multitude of ways of coming to know those principles even for those whose deepest reason for abiding by them is religious.

In the domain of ethics, then, religious commitment to classical theism neither unduly narrows one's theoretical and normative choices, nor necessarily leads to judgments or conduct whose rationality is suspect even on the most rigorously secular grounds. This point is important for understanding the political philosophy to be partially set out in this book. That position can play the positive role it is intended to play in contributing to the flourishing of democracy only if religious citizens can see how, given the autonomy of ethics, the position can still fully accommodate them. That it can do so will be shown in the next two chapters.

CHAPTER 2

THE LIBERTY OF CITIZENS AND THE RESPONSIBILITIES OF GOVERNMENT

Democracy is often characterized as a kind of government of, by, and for the people. A great deal of content is implicit in these monosyllables. The "of" indicates that the people are the governed and suggests that those who govern come from among them and live equally under the law. The "by" indicates not only that those who govern come from among the people as opposed to, for instance, a hereditary monarchy or foreign power, but also have been freely elected and are subject to being voted out of office. The "for" is—or is best understood as—a rough equivalent of "for the benefit of." This gives the triad normative content: the kind of benefit in question is not merely economic or sociological; it includes well-being in the sense associated with the common good.

If a democracy is indeed a political system in which government is of, by, and for the people as I have portrayed that, we can readily see that it requires both liberty and a certain kind of basic political equality. Without liberty, people cannot truly govern themselves, and they would likely be at best agents of others who control them. Without a kind of basic political equality, one that minimally embodies a commitment to one person, one vote, "the people" would not truly govern themselves. Liberty, including religious liberty, and basic political equality are morally cogent ideals in any case. What *degree* of religious freedom should be legally permissible and how the state should protect it are quite different matters.

Where there is liberty, there is room for pluralism. Where sociocultural life is complex, liberty virtually guarantees a high degree of pluralism. This is not to say that *fostering* pluralism is intrinsic to a sound democratic system of government, though a case can be made for that view, and *welcoming* pluralism *is* intrinsic to such a system. Whatever the prospects for such a case, my interest is in highly pluralistic democracies, which we find in much of the world today. Moreover, it is religious pluralism—including secular citizens as constituting one among the religiously plural groups—that most interests me here.

The framework this book presupposes is that of democracies which—even if, as a matter of historical precedent, they have an established church—are secular. Contemporary democratic states tend to be substantially secular in the sense that their legal and institutional framework exhibits separation of church and state in the sense required by three separationist principles that will be formulated and discussed in Section I. A democratic state should protect the liberty of its citizens and, in part for this reason, should accommodate both religious liberty and diversity in religion and in other realms of life. Religious citizens, however, commonly see a secular state as unfriendly toward religion. A major question underlying this chapter is how secular governments should provide for the liberty of all in a way that observes a reasonable separation of church and state and minimizes alienation of religious citizens. My thesis (in part) is that the optimal balance between secularity in the state and religiously motivated conduct on the part of many citizens requires both governmental adherence to institutional principles, such as those appropriate to a constitution, and citizens' adherence to principles of civic virtue that apply to individual conduct. The former are the main subject of this chapter, the latter the main subject of the next.

I. The Separation of Church and State and
the Limits of Democratic Authority

I assume that an appropriate church-state separation is a protection of both religious liberty and governmental autonomy. It is also required by any sound theory of democratic authority. What I call democratic authority is not the de facto power of the citizens in a democracy to determine its policies by enforcing the will of the majority. This is democratic *power*. I understand democratic authority normatively: roughly as the moral right of citizens in a democracy to exercise power—within certain limits. The basis of this right is a major issue in political philosophy and cannot be pursued in detail here. There is fairly widespread agreement that citizens normally have such a right if their government—through which they must exercise it—is both freely elected by them ("legitimate," in one sense) and, often enough, adequately reflects their will in its policies.[1] Democratic legitimacy as I understand it presupposes that democracy is a morally acceptable form of government in the first place and is "of, by, and for the people" in a sense entailing that it is duly elected by the people, adequately responsive to their will, and committed to enhancement of the well-being of the populace.[2]

This separation of church and state is a major element in the limitation of democratic authority. One reason for the enormous importance of that separation is that protection of religious liberty is clearly a condition for the moral acceptability of a government, and where church and state are not separate, religious liberty is threatened. Religious minorities— including the non-religious—may reasonably fear, if not domination by the majority religion, then at least discrimination favoring that. The religious majority itself may reasonably fear domination or undue influence by government officials whether they are religious or not. Political power need not align with religious ideals even when it countenances an established church; an established church may not be faithful to its own religious ideals even when it wears the mantle of political power.

Separation of church and state is most commonly considered in relation to restricting governmental activity toward religion. We may also take the separation more broadly, as calling for some restriction of the activities of churches toward government. That facet of separation will be considered in Chapter 3. As to governmental regulation and structure, three major principles I defend are these. The first is a liberty principle, which requires government to protect religious liberty. The second is an equality principle, which requires its equal treatment of different religions. The third is a neutrality principle, which requires governmental neutrality toward religion.

II. The Liberty Principle and the Scope of Religious Freedom

I have said that socioculturally complex societies tend to be pluralistic. Pluralism, especially in institutions and intellectual outlook, may well tend to strengthen democracy, if only by bringing together different points of view and generating debate and competition among them. Pluralism can also lead to fragmentation and sectarian strife, but it need not do so and is less likely to do so *given* appropriate legal and cultural circumstances. Whatever the prospects for showing that pluralism supports democracy, my interest is in highly pluralistic democracies such as we find in much of the world today.

Coercion is of special concern, in and quite apart from democratic societies, for at least two reasons. First, it negates liberty: what we are coerced to do we do not freely do. Second, it creates inequality; insofar as one person exercises coercive power over another, the latter is not the equal of the former. Moreover, liberty and a kind of basic political equality are the (normative) default position in democracies—at least in the liberal kind of interest here—and one implication of this point is that government, even more than individuals, should coercively restrict the liberty of citizens only on the basis of adequate justification.

Does this also hold for residents who are non-citizens? Much of the world is now experiencing illegal immigration, and many countries have legal aliens who do not have the legal rights of citizens. A full theory of the justification of governmental coercion must take account of the rights of these residents, but here it will suffice to focus on citizens as the central concern of the theory of government and to suggest that, other things equal (as admittedly they often will not be), legal residents should have the liberties and most other rights of citizens.

The scope of governmental power over the governed is plausibly thought to be limited by what is commonly called "the harm principle," famously formulated by J. S. Mill in *On Liberty*:

> The object of this Essay is to assert one very simple principle, as entitled to govern absolutely the dealings of society with the individual in the way of compulsion and control . . . That principle is, that the sole end for which mankind are warranted, individually or collectively, in interfering with the liberty of action of any of their number, is self-protection . . . to prevent harm to others.[3]

This principle is essential in what I call *the liberty principle*—that government should protect religious liberty to the highest degree possible within a reasonable interpretation of the harm principle. The liberty principle is implicit in the standards for freedom of action, conscience, and thought essential for a sound democracy. The appropriate scope of liberty has been extensively discussed, and here I will simply record sympathy with the idea, defended in *On Liberty* and a multitude of writings following it, that justification of restrictions of liberty must come from adequate evidence that non-restriction will be significantly harmful to persons—though I would add that harm to animals, the environment, or even property should also be taken to be a potentially adequate ground for restricting liberty.

Since liberty in general, and not just in religious conduct, is a constitutive standard in a sound democracy, one might ask what is special about religious liberty. I have said that the harm principle (properly interpreted) is important for any sound democracy. Why should religion be singled out in this connection? We could indeed simply discuss what harms justify what restrictions of the behavior that causes them, but we would quickly find that religious people—and many non-religious fellow citizens—feel strongly that religious liberty is one of the most important kinds needing protection.

There are historical reasons for special attention to religion in political philosophy. One is the enormous power that religions—and sometimes clergy as individuals—have had over the faithful. Faced with the threat of death if they do not do something and the lure of heaven if they do, they may be so powerfully motivated as to kill, or die, for their cause. There is also a reason that is quite different and may be only indirectly connected with preventing manipulation of citizens. I have in mind a principle applicable to church and state alike:

> *The protection of identity principle.* The deeper a set of commitments is in a person, and the closer it comes to determining that person's sense of identity, the stronger the case for protecting the expression of those commitments tends to be.

This principle is religiously neutral in content; but, as a matter of historical fact and perhaps of human psychology as well, religious commitments tend to be important for people in both ways: in depth and in determining the sense of identity. Other kinds of commitments can be comparably deep; this principle does not discriminate against those. But few if any non-religious kinds of commitments combine the depth and contribution to the sense of identity that go with many (though not all) of the kinds of religious commitments.

III. The Equality Principle and the Case against Establishment

The equality principle implies non-establishment as ordinarily understood: minimally, as requiring that no religion has official state endorsement and a statutory role in legislation or in determining public policy. Suppose, however, that all religions had a common element and establishing a religion built solely on this element is possible. Then a *limited* kind of establishment might be consistent with the equality principle, which requires government to treat all religions equally. The establishment would be limited in part because the common element might be major in one religion and minor in another. The common religion would thus better represent some religions than others, and establishing it might at best achieve a kind of proportionate equality in which members of some religious groups might properly feel like second-class citizens.

There are also kinds of establishment that are independent of the content of the religion being established. Two kinds in particular should be distinguished. *Formal establishment* occurs when (as in England) there is a statutory or broadly constitutional governmental role for a particular religion. In a weak version, formal establishment simply provides for guaranteed *representation* of a particular religion in one or more governmental institutions: no governmental powers are conferred, as opposed to, say, limited observer status, or at most non-voting membership in, a parliamentary body. In any case, formal establishment does not imply *doctrinal establishment*, which occurs when certain substantive religious doctrines (say about the meaning of marriage and the rights pertaining to it) are given a specific role in law or public policy.[4]

Doctrinal establishment may exist in degrees: its extent is proportional to the power of the established church and the strength of the specifically religious doctrines built into the role the established religion plays. If, moreover, a specific denomination is established, this represents a higher degree of establishment than where only a much wider institutional and doctrinal framework, say Christianity, is established; and if, by contrast, only "civil religion" is established, the degree is lower still.[5]

Formal establishment is possible even where the religious officials in question are committed to exercising governmental influence only where it meets non-religious criteria for benefiting the populace a whole.[6] Doctrinal establishment may imply governmental support for special privileges, say in higher education, for members of the established church. But its strength will vary with the doctrines, especially those constituting a moral or political view, characteristic of the religion in question. Formal establishment may, in a given state, produce a measure of doctrinal establishment, but need not, and doctrinal establishment may, depending on the religion in question, have little or no effect on governmental policy. For these reasons, it is a contingent matter whether establishment results in unjustified restrictions of liberty or is simply a matter of special representation by one segment of the population—such representation may or may not coincide with the will of the great majority of citizens.

My position, however, implies that even merely formal establishment constitutes a liability to unjustified governmental restrictions of liberty and is at least unharmonious with the equal treatment of religions—and of citizens themselves—which is an ideal of democracy. As long as there are secular citizens—or indeed there is freedom for religious citizens to become secular—establishment tends to give preference to religious over secular citizens. This holds even in the unlikely event that there is a limited kind of establishment under which government treats all religions equally. These and other points indicate reasons for adopting the neutrality principle.

IV. The Neutrality Principle: Accommodationist Secularity

The neutrality principle, which calls for governmental neutrality toward religion and the religious, is not entailed by even the other two principles together nor, so far as I know, clearly required by the U.S. Constitution. In political philosophy it is also more controversial. Much more could be said about each, but here a few further clarifications must suffice.

Neutrality is best understood in the context of a governmental commitment to liberty, in part because government should not be neutral toward either threats to liberty or violations of liberties guaranteed by law. This, in turn, is because liberty is a constitutive standard in any morally sound democracy and certainly in any liberal democracy, a kind in which, as on Mill's conception, a commitment to preservation of a kind of maximal liberty is a basic structural element. But liberty cannot be unlimited. Justified limitations are determined by moral considerations such as human rights. We need not take rights as morally basic. Whether we appeal to rights or not, the appropriate limitations would imply the moral wrongness of certain extreme forms of religious conduct, any kind that, like ritual human sacrifice and ceremonial mutilation of children, violates clearly reasonable standards for the protection of persons.[7] Even non-violent mistreatment reatment of women and, especially, children may be justifiably prohibited by law. Children should not be forced, under religiously protected parental powers, to marry while they are in their early teens to mid-teens, as the State of Texas took to occur in a Mormon community raided by Texas authorities in the spring of 2008.

Such limitations on protection of religious liberty also illustrate the limited governmental neutrality toward religion which defenders of liberal democracy have generally endorsed. Proper protections of religious liberty provide for great diversity in styles of life but prohibit (non-self-defensive) harms to other persons. Nonetheless, certain restrictions of religious liberty that involve only standards of dress may be warranted. Consider the possibility that certain garments would be dangerous in a factory where they might be caught in machinery.

The questions raised recently in France concerning dress codes for students and, in Turkey, concerning the propriety of head scarves for women are different and more controversial. We can say, however, that the mere fact that a mode of dress is not a direct harm to anyone does not imply that government has no justification for restricting it in public or on government property. There are not only considerations of security but also considerations of appropriateness in public places. These considerations should not be designed or interpreted so as to favor any one group, as where a large majority is permitted to wear clothing prominently representing a single religion that is openly hostile to those outside it. The case for restraint, however, should—as is required by the protection of identity principle—be stronger in proportion to the importance of the mode of dress for the religious citizens in question.

As these points indicate, equality must be understood to allow differential treatment of citizens provided its basis is non-religious and otherwise justified. Consider, for instance, the practice, in many countries, of having state holidays on Christian (or Muslim or Jewish) feast days. This may in fact advantage Christians, but may be justifiably maintained on the ground that it well serves a majority of the population, not because that majority is Christian. The governmental policy in question might equally have benefited some other religious group. Differential effect does not entail structural bias. The point to be added here is one that the equality principle implies. Minority religious groups should, within practicable limits, have comparable leave for their religious observances, particularly in government employment.

Even religious freedom and governmental neutrality toward religion, then, *may* be limited in some ways in a morally sound democracy that is appropriately neutral in matters of religion. This point is probably uncontroversial, but there is disagreement concerning the degree to which a democracy may *promote* the practice of religion as such, provided it does not prefer one religion over another.[8] Suppose that a majority of the people want compulsory religious services—though without favoring any domination—in the schools. Why is this an objectionable exercise of democratic authority?

One might compare this policy with government's providing (as in some European countries) for religious children to receive religious instruction (as distinct from religious services) only in their own denominations and by people approved by authorities in those denominations. On that model, schools might also provide, for the religious and non-religious alike, periods of meditation that, being without content requirements, are essentially secular. Nonetheless, this second policy might benefit religious students in a way it does not benefit secular ones, who would tend to treat the occasions differently (e.g., not for prayer) and more often seek excuses for absence. It would not, however, make the latter *conspicuously* absent, as they would often be from even voluntary religious observances, which they might find alien or even quite unpleasant. Even if prejudice does not arise, the result of any of these policies might be polarizing, particularly where students may choose among services in a denominational religion like Christianity, in which some denominations might compete with others for adherents. A policy of required services, even with meditation as an alternative, differs, then, from required religious education. It is true that, indirectly, the latter can differentially benefit the religious, if only by promoting understanding of the various religions studied and thereby limiting prejudice or, in some cases, exposing secular students to some of their attractive elements that can enter the curriculum without endorsement. Such contingent benefits to some subgroup of the population may be intrinsic to pluralistic democracies. This issue will be shortly discussed further when we consider the case for educational vouchers.

V. Religious Neutrality, Valuational Neutrality, and Public Policy

Neutrality toward religion presents a definition problem even apart from the difficulty of defining 'religion.' Two points and an example will add clarity. First, neutrality does not imply indifference. Indeed, religious liberty is an important kind and governments should solicitously preserve it. Second, as noted already, governmental neutrality toward religion does not prevent contingent circumstances from causing religious institutions to benefit from laws or policies instituted by government. Let me illustrate this.

Religious Neutrality in Science Education

Consider science education. Government may (given sufficient support from the scientific community) require teaching evolutionary biology in public school science—even in required science courses that expose all students to the teaching—despite some religious parents' contending that this infringes on their religious liberty to bring up their children believing in, say, creationism. To be sure, democratic governments may not properly sponsor hostility to religion, any more than they may sponsor religion itself; but that does not preclude teaching, as true or highly confirmed, a theory that denies some scriptural claims. Teaching evolutionary theory as true does not (at least for all versions of that theory) imply any metaphysical claims, including any denial of the claim that the physical world was created by God and remains under divine sovereignty.[9] Scientific inquiry does not require assuming either that God did or that God did not create the universe with all the laws and elements constituting subject matter for scientific explanations and theories.

The rigorous practice of science should not be seen as necessarily in tension with a religious view of the world. Some religious views simply do not imply any claims that are inconsistent with scientifically well-confirmed propositions; and, as appropriately practiced, science—as opposed to certain philosophical interpretations of it—does not imply metaphysical claims about, for instance, the origin of the universe. One can be scientifically rigorous in studying the natural world without commitment to any specific propositions about the supernatural. Seeking explanations of natural events in terms of descriptive categories of natural science (especially physics, chemistry, and biology) leaves open what other realities there might be. Positing divine creation and divine sovereignty leaves open what scientific inquiry may discover about the course of nature.

In many religious traditions, including at least Christianity and Judaism, the scientific study of nature is readily viewed as an attempt to understand God's creation. One can view scientific inquiry as a use of reason conceived as a natural endowment from God. To be sure, the theory of evolution is inconsistent with the account of creation given in Genesis interpreted *literally*. But literal interpretation of scripture throughout is not a requirement of a reasonable theology and is increasingly rejected by educated Biblical interpreters. This is not to deny that there can be tension between scientific results and some scripturally based beliefs on the part of a religiously committed person. The point is that it is theologically implausible to think of scripture as competing with scientific inquiry with respect to answering the same questions. One possibility, for instance, is to take the account in Genesis to be affirming (among other things, to be sure) the creative action and sovereignty of God. These generic attributions are compatible with the theory of evolution.[10]

The neutrality principle must not be given either of two overbroad interpretations. First, neutrality toward the truth of religious doctrines does not imply that the state must consider religion undeserving of a place in the required curriculum. Not to teach *about* religion, historically and sociologically for instance, would be a drastic mistake, but one can teach about its content, development, and influence in, say, a history or literature class without endorsing or denying religious propositions. To be sure, doctrinal neutrality is compatible with attitudinal hostility. That hostility toward religion is offensive to many citizens and inappropriate to teaching about religion. Second, despite the close association between religion and ethics and the common view that ethical principles depend for their "validity" on religion (or at least on the existence of God), teaching ethics need not violate the neutrality principle. Consider teaching the kind of common-sense ethical principles expressed in the major ethical theories and indeed in the ethical (non-theological) Ten Commandments, including the prohibitions of killing, stealing, and lying. Given the epistemic autonomy of ethics explained in Chapter 1, it should be clear how theists—even those holding certain divine command views in ethics—can without impiety teach moral principles stated non-religiously and can indeed do so essentially as secular colleagues would.

By contrast, the neutrality principle does preclude public schools' teaching creationism, which explicitly says that God created human beings, as a true position, since that would endorse a religious view. The equality principle would also preclude doing this if (as is possible) some religion denies God's creating the world, since one could not then teach it without disfavoring that religion. Neither the equality nor the neutrality principle, however, precludes noncommittally mentioning creationism. Nonetheless, doing this is neither necessary for good science teaching nor likely to be welcome to students and parents who wish the view to be presented as credible. So presenting it would be beyond the capacity, and would certainly evoke the disapproval, of many science teachers.

If neutrality precludes teaching creationism, it also precludes *denying* such religious propositions as that God created the world. Doing this might also be precluded by the liberty principle on the ground that it tends to reduce religious liberty, but certain kinds of denial need not have this tendency. In any case, to see the scope of neutrality, we need a good understanding of what constitutes denial. I take the basic case of denying a proposition—*direct denial*—to be either asserting that it is false or affirming its negation. We should also recognize *indirect denial*. This might be equivalent to an assertion that is not a denial but does self-evidently and obviously entail a denial. Suppose a teacher said that if God, as all-knowing, all-powerful, and perfectly good, created humanity, people would be less prone to evil than they are. Any normal adolescent could see this to imply that it is not true that God created humanity. It would not be a religiously neutral assertion.

The issue becomes more complex when the non-neutral implication is not obvious or self-evident, but is ascertainable by reflection on the part of a normal adult with at least the level of education reasonably aimed at for students in (say) the tenth grade or above. Imagine that a teacher considers a version of "intelligent design" theory and composes a list of apparent evidences of divine action in the genesis of humanity. The teacher indicates that the list includes all the possible kinds of evidence and then presents data in such a way as to yield a series of arguments, one marshaling each kind of evidence, and each concluding that the relevant evidence is missing. At the end of this process, for instance after half a dozen arguments are mounted, the teacher might say that we cannot rationally believe a claim for which there is no relevant evidence. Doing this may seem an *implicit denial* of the religious proposition (in this case, the proposition that there has been divine action in the genesis of humanity); but it does not carry a commitment to deeming the proposition *false*. It is, however, an *implicit rejection*—representing the proposition as unworthy of belief.[11]

It will be no surprise that there are borderline cases. Suppose the teacher had concluded instead that there is no evidence of divine creation of humanity and that the probability of such creation is very low. This is not neutral toward religion but is not a clear case of denying the religious view in question. If the teacher had simply said there is no evidence (scientific or other), we would not have denial, but would still have a breach of neutrality. Implying that there is no *non*-scientific evidence for theism (such as evidence from personal religious experience) is neither neutral toward religion nor appropriate to the teaching of science. Breach of neutrality, then, does not entail denial of a religious view. This makes neutrality more difficult to achieve. Two points must be added immediately.

First, just as breach of neutrality does not entail denial of a religious view, the latter—for one broad and common notion of denying a religious view—does not entail breach of neutrality toward religion. There are many statements in the Bible that are denied—if taken literally as descriptions of fact—by religious people whose mode of Biblical interpretation makes frequent appeal to symbolism, metaphor, and the ways of narrative. Some people may think that any serious cosmic or ethical pronouncements by certain religious authorities are religious statements. The second point, then, is that it would be a mistake to define neutrality toward religion so broadly that denial of any such statement entails breaching neutrality. Doing so might also be plausibly considered favoritism toward, hence a failure of neutrality toward, religion.

State neutrality toward religion in the sense in which it is a sound political ideal, then, does not entail neutrality regarding every possible religion or every statement deemed religious. Given that almost any statement can be deemed religious by someone, and that religious institutions can be built around indefinitely many sets of statements and practices, to require such sweeping neutrality would make unreasonable demands on both government in general and education in particular.

Neutrality in Matters of Value

Given that for some political philosophers (notably Rawls), liberal democracy should be neutral toward "comprehensive" views of the good, such as Judaism, Christianity, or Islam on the religious side and, on the ethics side, Kantianism and utilitarianism.[12] It should be stressed that the kind of governmental neutrality I support is not *value*-neutrality. This includes neutrality both toward what has value in itself and is thus a proper object of basic concern and neutrality toward specific moral principles that go beyond the general normative standards that Rawls and a number of other liberal theorists take to be needed for democratic societies. This valuational element in my view is evident even in relation to the kinds of moral considerations that, for any sound democracy, figure in restricting liberty. As illustrated already, these involve a notion of harm. Thus, even on a negative conception of morality according to which its concern is only to prevent harm, we would still need an account of harms or of some still wider range of evils whose prevention can justify limitations on the freedom of citizens. For liberal democracy is clearly committed to supporting the maximal liberty that citizens can exercise without producing certain harms (or a substantial likelihood of them). Thus, even if a liberal state could be neutral toward the good, it could not be neutral toward the bad. It could not be value-neutral.

We cannot sharply distinguish, however, between a government's restricting liberty as a way to prevent harm and its doing so as a way of promoting some good. Compulsory education— a major but uncontroversial limitation of liberty in democratic societies—is essential to prevent the harms that ignorance is likely to cause. These include liability to political manipulation by demagogues as well as dangers to the physical or psychological health of the population. But even apart from the prevention of certain harms as essential in guiding compulsory education, promoting certain goods is implicit in properly structuring the curriculum. Education itself is surely one kind of good, and in practice it is impossible to educate in a way that is effective in preventing harm yet is not, in the main, inherently good. These points are illustrated by competent teaching of history, literature, and science, among other subjects. Both the education provided by such teaching and the activity of competently teaching them are inherently good. Moreover, at least where it is the liberty of children that is restricted, considerations of what is for their good, as opposed to preventing harms to them, may carry substantial weight. These considerations may certainly carry such weight in choosing among different ways in which children's liberty may be restricted to avoid harm to them. (A parallel to this second point appears to hold for the case of adults, but further discussion of this matter is not necessary here.)

Educational Vouchers and Governmental Neutrality

We might clarify neutrality further in relation to educational vouchers. Vouchers provide funds for parents to educate their children in schools of their choice—religious or secular. Their justification given church-state separation has been contested in the United States for reasons that apply to democratic societies worldwide.[13] Vouchers may be viewed in relation to all three principles of church-state separation proposed here, but are especially relevant to understanding governmental neutrality. There is no question that vouchers may differentially benefit the religious. But they are not defined in a way that favors religious over non-religious citizens, nor are voucher programs necessarily addressed to religious citizens, as opposed to citizens who simply wish to have educational choices beyond the public school system.

The issue of voucher legislation is at a different level from that of the three church-state separation principles. Not only is it far more specific and not of a broadly constitutional kind; a voucher program is also implicitly addressed to parents and guardians rather than to government and citizens generally. Still, this difference in addressees does not undermine a significant similarity between a voucher program and the separation principles. All four them are defensible on the basis of non-religious considerations, as already shown for the separation principles. In the case of vouchers, a secular reason—say that respect for religious and other liberties requires legalizing vouchers—is central. What this indicates is that a non-religious reason need not be secular in its *content,* as opposed to its evidential *grounds.* That religious liberty should be protected is a conclusion one may come to quite apart from having any religious commitments.

Voucher programs should be compared with "faith-based initiatives," under which government may fund civic activities, such as services to the poor, that are provided by one or another religiously affiliated organization. Here governments, as opposed to parents, choose what organizations are to receive funds—a policy that might give government inappropriate power over religion. If, however, governments fund religious organizations through a fair competition with secular ones, the program need not violate the equality principle; and it is arguable that *not* allowing religious organizations to compete for funds here would abridge their liberty, at least in making them ineligible for a significant kind of expression of their ideals.

As to the neutrality principle, if the faith-based activities in question are both needed (as with education) and not designed to favor the capacities of religious organizations, the principle might allow government funding of certain programs carried out by those organizations. But even if there need be no governmental favoritism of religious organizations, its effect of such funding might be to promote them significantly more than their secular counterparts. For one thing, they might simply emerge more successfully from the fair competition. More important, their own religious missions could be significantly advanced—and more so than those of their secular competitors—as a collateral effect of their governmentally approved work. This collateral benefit might to some people seem a sufficient reason to prohibit governmental funding of religious organizations, but a good case can be made that this prohibition neither treats them equally with secular organizations nor adequately serves the public.[14]

The wisdom of providing vouchers is an issue that goes beyond separation of church and state. One question is whether completely neutral governments can adequately provide for religious liberty *within* public schools. On one view, complete neutrality would imply restricting religious expression during school hours and a good remedy for such restrictions is for governments to provide, as in some European countries, denominational instruction for students who wish it, while matching the time period and educational service with suitable offerings for secular students. If, however, students have freedom of speech and also some free time for unobtrusive religious observations, it is arguable that this suffices for the religious liberty during school attendance. I leave this issue open.

I also leave open the question whether a voucher system would weaken the public school system, if only by reducing available funds below an acceptable threshold. It might be argued, however, that by suitably examining students and inspecting all schools, government can guarantee educational quality in both public schools and those qualifying for vouchers. Enhancing private education might encourage pluralism, but it might also lead to sectarian or class divisions that are inimical to the health of a democracy. There are further issues that must be addressed for a full assessment of the wisdom of a voucher system, but enough has been said to show that a reasonable church-state separation may well be compatible with providing vouchers under carefully defined conditions.

———

Given what we have seen concerning the moral constraints on democracy as a form of government, it seems clear that the liberty, equality, and neutrality principles should be part of its framework. These cannot be precisely defined, but liberty should be as extensive as it can be within the limits of a plausible interpretation of the harm principle. Equal treatment of different religions should be a guide to lawmaking and public policy; but, owing to inevitable contingencies in civic life, it cannot be guaranteed not to have a differential and sometimes beneficial effect on one or another religion. Governmental neutrality toward religion and the religious is also important; but it cannot be absolute, and even when it is scrupulously observed it does not imply neutrality in matters of value. Judgments of what is worthwhile in human life are essential for properly determining the content and manner of required public education. The kinds of values that government may presuppose—including not only liberty and equality but also elements of human flourishing—may be favored more by some religions than by others. But where citizens understand the basic principles of sound democratic governance, it will be clear that even the best governments cannot expect to win the approval of every citizen. It is enough that the framework of a sound democracy provides opportunities for every citizen to protest and to seek support for rectifying inequalities that historical contingencies may bring.

CHAPTER 3

THE SECULAR STATE AND THE RELIGIOUS CITIZEN

It should now be clear that an appropriate church-state separation is a protection of both religious liberty and governmental autonomy. This separation is most commonly considered in relation to restricting governmental activity toward religion. We may also take the separation more broadly, as calling for some restriction of the activities of churches toward government. That facet of separation will also be explored. As to governmental regulation and structure, the principles I have defended—a liberty principle, which requires government to protect religious liberty; an equality principle, which requires its equal treatment of different religions; and a neutrality principle, which requires governmental neutrality toward religion—will serve as a framework.

I. Freedom of Expression in the Advocacy of Laws and Public Policies

The liberty, equality, and neutrality principles apply to democracies in general, but so far I have focused on laws and public policies and on the principles of governmental conduct that are most needed for preserving a reasonable church-state separation. These three principles apply to governmental laws and policies relating to free expression—whether to protecting it or to limiting it—as well as to other kinds of governmental laws and policies. Free expression, however, may have many purposes other than advocacy of laws or public policies, and most of it is neither governmental nor political. In both instances—those of advocacy or other support of laws or public policies and those of free expression with no such purpose—I am assuming that democracies should recognize a moral right to "maximal" freedom of expression in public discourse, and that here, as in other realms of conduct, liberty is the default position.

In the governmental regulatory activities of any sound democracy, the state must justify restrictions of liberty, especially of thought, expression, and free association in cooperative enterprises. Permitting such "natural" liberties as freedom of movement and of personal association does not normally need justification. Indeed, many other liberties can be argued to be implicit in these natural ones, certainly including liberties of thought, expression, and association. There is no need here to classify liberties further; the protections of liberty crucial for a sound democracy are highly comprehensive.

Those engaging in free expression need not have any particular purpose in expressing themselves. More important for this book, their speaking and writing need not be political and certainly need not aim at coercion or even persuasion. By contrast, advocacy of laws or public policies normally is intended to persuade or even compel, and most laws and public policies are also coercive. Moreover, supporting laws or public policies by voting to institute them is commonly intended to require conformity to them on pain of legal penalty. Such legal requirement is a form of coercion. For coercion of others, as opposed to free expression of our thoughts and feelings, we should meet higher standards—both moral and legal—than for free expression in general. We are morally free, and should be legally free, to seek to *persuade* others to do things we ought not to *coerce* them to do, whether the coercion is by legal or other means.

Rights, Obligations, and Responsibilities

The distinction between persuasion and coercion is of great importance in political philosophy. Related to it is another distinction: in the moral as well as the political realm, it is essential to distinguish *rights* from *oughts*. There are things many of us ought to do, from deeds as deliberate as giving to charity to simple services like removing sharp roofing nails from a driveway we are crossing, which we nonetheless have a moral right *not* to do. No one may coerce charitable contributions or even properly assert that financially able non-contributors have violated the rights of charities or their beneficiaries. Charities have a right to *request* contributions (in appropriate ways); they do not have a right to our actually contributing, even if this is something that, as responsible citizens in a world with widespread poverty, we ought to do.

It is an important point about just laws that they do not prohibit conduct to which there is a moral right. It is also important—but less often emphasized—that even a comprehensive system of just laws does not require of citizens everything that citizens morally ought to do. Much of what we ought to do lies in the realm of private voluntary conduct, say interactions between spouses or friends. Morality does not just protect our liberty; it also guides our discretion.

Another way to see how rights differ from oughts is to note that the latter, but not the former, imply reasons for action. Whereas, for what we morally ought to do, we have a *reason*—having a right to do something does not imply having any reason to do it. The right to abstain from giving to charity illustrates this. It is, moreover, a right that the prosperous should not exercise. Another example concerns ordinary cooperative activities: I have a right to raise my hand and speak in a meeting I am in, but this gives me no reason to do so. Indeed, I ought not to exercise the right if I lack a legitimate purpose. The point is not that rights have no connection with reasons; *others* have a reason not to prevent my exercise of my rights. Rights, then, do not confer on their possessor any reason to do what they protect, but they do impose reasons on their addressees not to prevent the protected actions.

Legal versus Ethical Constraints

I would argue (as would many others) that given our moral rights, free expression and advocacy should be *legally* limited only by a harm principle roughly to the effect that the liberty of competent adults should be restricted only to prevent harm to other people, animals, or the environment (normally in that order of priority, and including damage to certain property as an indirect harm to persons, though to say this is not to establish any specific weighting of harms in one of the categories against harms in either of the others). *Ethically*, however, both free expression and advocacy—and especially advocacy of coercive laws and public policies—should meet standards higher than this very permissive legal one. Legally, one might permissibly support an immoral cause, say lifting perfectly just regulation of an industry that pollutes the environment but in which one has a personal interest, or supporting an oppressive foreign regime where one's only reason is personal financial gain. Morally, one should not do these things.

That the scope of morality is wider than that determined by legal and even moral rights is a point supported by any plausible virtue ethics. Virtue calls for seeking excellence; and even where we do not approach ethical ideals—say in such interpersonal virtues as beneficence, fidelity, and sincerity—we would be ethically deficient in relation to those virtues if we did no more than we must to stay within our rights. As our examples show, however, the point is plausible quite apart from the case for virtue ethics. The next section will propose and defend some principles expressing such higher standards, and the concluding section will take up ethical standards concerning free expression with content that does not support coercion.

II. Major Principles Governing the Advocacy of Laws and Public Policies

Regarding the ethics of good citizenship, many principles have been proposed. The most plausible ones embody some notion of the kinds of reasons citizens in democracies should take as a basis of political decisions and especially for votes. The appropriate reasons may also be called public, secular, or evidentially adequate. Some of the best-known principles come from Rawls. He has said, for instance,

> [P]ublic reason is the sole reason the court exercises. It is the only branch of government that is visibly on its face the creature of that reason . . . Citizens and legislators may properly vote their more comprehensive [e.g. religious] views when constitutional essentials and basic justice are not at stake.[1]

Rawls has qualified this standard in ways that complicate assessment of his view. In the same lecture he adds, to a formulation of this standard, "provided they do this [vote their comprehensive views] in ways that strengthen the ideal of public reason itself."[2] By contrast, in the Preface to a later version of the same book, he says that reasonable comprehensive doctrines "may be introduced in public reason at any time provided that in due course public reasons, given by a reasonable political conception, are presented sufficient to support whatever the comprehensive doctrines are introduced to support."[3]

Rawls's earlier principle is representative of what is perhaps his most influential work on the topic, but I cannot discuss the many subtleties of his position. What should be said now is that his later proviso, even though restricted to "reasonable" comprehensive views, is seriously indeterminate. Take the claim that such views (which include religious doctrines) "may be introduced in public reason at any time." This may well be at the time of a legislative decision and may then determine law or public policy. That possibility makes doubly important the constraint that "in due course public reasons, given by a reasonable political conception, are presented sufficient to support whatever the comprehensive doctrines are introduced to support." One problem is that due course may be easily taken to be years and—more important—can apparently be long enough for enactment to occur or even take effect and perhaps become entrenched. Even when a law or policy is not entrenched, reversal may be unfeasible or politically difficult.

A quite different problem is that it is also doubtful that one can conscientiously claim that public reasons will be available when one does not have them at least in outline at the time. Anticipating them is not like predicting, say, population expansion, where we may be guided by hard data and well-confirmed theory. Particularly where one's reason for coercion is religious, how can one reasonably predict that adequate public reason, though evading one's serious reflection now, will be found? This problem seems intractable; and, added to the vagueness of "due course," it indicates that the proviso is not a desirable qualification of Rawls's earlier view.

A plausible and quite different standard has been proposed by Kent Greenawalt:

> Legislation must be justified in terms of secular objectives, but when people reasonably think that shared premises of justice and criteria for determining truth cannot resolve critical questions of fact, fundamental questions of value, or the weighing of competing benefits and harms, they do properly rely on religious convictions that help them answer these questions.[4]

This is permissive in one way—sometimes allowing religious convictions to determine law and policy without restriction on content or source—but quite demanding in another. It requires a *reasonable* judgment that shared premises cannot resolve the relevant question; and it suggests that, when it comes to passing legislation, justification by secular reasons should be available. I take this to mean, not available "in due course," but rather, cited at the time of advocacy.

More permissive toward the propriety of basing political decisions on religious reasons is Weithman's view:

> Citizens of a liberal democracy may base their votes on reasons drawn from their comprehensive moral views, including their religious views, without having other reasons which are sufficient for their vote—provided they sincerely believe that their government would be justified in adopting the measures they vote for.[5]

On this view, legislators might not themselves have any secular reason at all, provided they believe that the measure they want their government to institute is justified. This gives them room to be (as Weithman would encourage) both rigorous and quite ecumenical—even secular—regarding what constitutes governmental justification; but it also allows them to take religious considerations to suffice at that level too. The proposed standard of justification may, as applied by some, be demanding; but being determined by what they believe, the standard is internal to their own, possibly sectarian, perspective.

My concern in this chapter is mainly with the ethics of citizenship in relation to religious and political matters. I am especially concerned with ethical constraints on coercion, as in legally restricting human conduct. With these matters in mind, I propose a principle that places a moderate limitation on sociopolitical appeals to religious reasons:

> *The principle of secular rationale.* Citizens in a democracy have a prima facie obligation not to advocate or support any law or public policy that restricts human conduct, unless they

have, and are willing to offer, adequate secular reason for
this advocacy or support (e.g. for a vote).[6]

This principle is probably more restrictive than any of the
above, except for Rawls's principle cited first—on the assumption that the laws in question, which restrict human conduct,
at least very commonly involve either what he calls "constitutional essentials" or basic justice, and so would fall under his
restrictions.[7] The secular rationale principle has been widely
misunderstood. Here are a few of the needed qualifications of
the principle and an indication of its basis.

A *prima facie obligation,* as illustrated by a number of our
examples, is one with a degree of normative force sufficient to
justify the act in question if there is no conflicting reason of at
least equal weight, but a prima facie reason is in a certain way
limited: the obligation is not absolute but *defeasible.* It may be
overridden by a competing obligation. Appeal to religious
considerations could, for instance, be necessary to gain sufficient support for enacting laws that will prevent a Nazi from
seizing power. Then one *should* appeal to them, though there
are appropriate and inappropriate ways to do so.

The prima facie obligation in question, like many other
prima facie obligations, is compatible with a *right to act otherwise.* The secular rationale standard is an element in good
citizenship; it need not be observed in merely permissible sociopolitical functioning in a free society. Here I must again
stress that there are wrongs within rights, and that I reject a
rights-based ethic on which our only moral obligations are to
avoid violating others' moral rights and, correspondingly, to
act within our own rights (though otherwise as we wish).

This is not to suggest that such a narrow, rights-based ethic
is widely held by ethical theorists; but the position is often presupposed for the special case of political conduct. On this,
many people may think that ethics has only the kind of negative bearing it does on the kind of proceduralist conception of

democracy that takes voting simply to establish majority preferences on which (within broad constitutional limits) government then acts. As support for my opposition to a rights-based
ethics, I have mentioned the wrongness of prosperous people's giving nothing to charity; some instances of withholding
support of public education would be another such case. In
personal relations, another instance would be ceasing to shovel
a bit more snow than legally required to clear a few feet of
sidewalk for an out-of town neighbor. In at least some such
cases, neighbors should do more than they have to. Think too,
of such virtues as generosity, kindness, and sociability, all of
which have sociopolitical counterparts. If one did for others as
little as one's rights allow, one would lead a self-centered existence that hovers somewhere between vice at the bottom and
mere decency at the top. If we all did that, life would be, if
bearable at all, far more difficult than it is.

A *secular reason* for an action (or a belief) is roughly one
whose status as a justifier of action (or belief) does not evidentially depend on (but also does not deny) the existence of
God; nor does it depend on theological considerations, or on
the pronouncements of a person or institution *as* a religious
authority. This notion is epistemic, roughly a matter of evidential grounding. It is not contentual, a matter of the content of
reasons: a secular reason may be to the effect that preservation
of governmental neutrality toward religion is desirable, and
here the notion of religion figures in the content of the
reason. Secular reasons for laws or public policies—say, considerations of public safety—will typically *accord* with reasons
that are supported by at least some major religion. Suppose
we have a religious obligation to promote human flourishing
in a sense requiring good health. This will generate a derivative obligation—prima facie but possibly strong—to support
public hygiene.

An *adequate reason* (for something) is one that, in rough
terms, evidentially justifies the belief, act, or other element it

supports. We might also say that adequacy implies that an action or belief based on the reason is thereby rational. The notions of justification and of adequacy are objective but complex and non-quantitative. There are degrees of justification, but in most contexts we cannot indicate them except by such terms as "minimally adequate (to justify)," "more than adequate," "compelling," and, where two independent considerations are in question, "a better reason (or justification) than the other." In many applications, the notion of an adequate reason is controversial, but no plausible political or legal philosophy can do without it or some equivalent. Secular reasons as here conceived are, at least when adequate, a species of natural reasons, an important category to be further clarified shortly.

Excusability also needs comment. It can explain why a person who does not live up to the principle of secular rationale is not ipso facto a "bad citizen." Like other failures, this one may be fully excusable. I think it often is, say where a person's upbringing and education create a religious bias the person cannot be reasonably expected to overcome in the circumstances. But conduct that is merely excusable is a kind we should try to avoid. Excusatory circumstances free us from blameworthiness, but they also reveal that apart from them we would have merited blame. Excusability is not a status to be aimed at, as is justification; but any theory of obligation or responsibility should take it into account. Excusability for not doing something, moreover, does not entail excusability for not trying.

The principle of secular rationale is *non-exclusive.* First, it does not rule out having *religious* reasons for legal coercion, nor imply that such reasons cannot have any justificatory power. Second, it does not even rule out having *only* religious reasons for lifting oppression or expanding *liberty*—which is not to say that there are no ethical or evidential standards applicable to so using such reasons. The principle concerns coercion, not behavior of just any kind; and it accords with the idea that freedom is the default position in a liberal democracy. Largely for that reason, it is a standard whose support may appropriately come from a wide variety of considerations. Third, it does not imply that religious reasons should be "privatized." Indeed, one might quite properly indicate, publicly, that one is supporting, say, illegalizing assisted suicide, *not* on religious grounds—for instance on the basis of reverence for God's gift of life—but for secular reasons, such as protection of vulnerable patients. A statement like this could have the double function both of indicating that one is religious and of communicating that one can act, and *is* acting, for non-religious reasons.

A quite different point is that the principle of secular rationale expresses a constraint on coercion, not a recommendation of when it should occur. The principle does not imply a positive obligation to institute laws or public policies whenever one *does* have adequate grounds from the point of view of natural reason. I have said that liberty is the default position in a sound democracy and should be protected unless there are adequate grounds for restricting it. But I do not hold that in every case in which those grounds are present, one must support the permissible restriction. The reasons for support may be just barely adequate to justify it. An adequate reason may suffice for justification without sufficing for wisdom. Think of gambling and of hunting: the first may harm innocent family members; the latter takes animal life. If the case for restriction is barely adequate, wisdom may favor legally preserving liberty and arguing for voluntary abstention.

The point that meeting a constraint does not entail that one should do the deed in question is not limited to the political domain. Justified conduct, when based on only minimally adequate reasons, may be more like criticizable action protected by rights than like desirable action called for by sound ideals. Persuasion may be a far better way to achieve an end that, even with ample justification, one could legally require, say (for the sake of argument) abstention from assisting with suicide. The general question here is when to prohibit as opposed to tolerating, given that both are justified. This question will be pursued in Chapter 4. Here we must still explore whether the principle of secular rationale can withstand recent criticisms.

III. The Charge of Exclusivism toward Religious Reasons

The principles defended in this book are elements in a kind of liberalism in political philosophy. Some critics of my view have charged that the liberalism in question, despite its substantially egalitarian aims, is insufficiently inclusive. This section responds to some representative critics.

Secularity, Scope of Acceptance, and Combinability of Reasons

A critical remark by Nicholas Wolterstorff provides an occasion for clarification. With my position as well as Rawls's and others in view, all of which he considers, "exclusivist," he says that "it is religious reasons that are to be excluded. But . . . that focus is entirely arbitrary. Any reason that is not shared by everybody is excluded."[8] I have explained why religious reasons are not excluded, though their use is constrained by the need for secular companions. I have not implied (and do not believe) that adequate reasons must be shared by everyone, even everyone who seriously considers them. They need only be in a certain way accessible to rational adults: roughly, appraisable by them through using natural reason in the light of facts to which they have access on the basis of exercising their natural rational capacities.

To be sure, where people are adequately informed of the relevant facts and fully rational, it is reasonable to expect them to *tend* to agree on whether a consideration is a reason for a law or public policy; but adequate information and full rationality are all too commonly not found together (and often neither is present—even allowing that full rationality need not be maximal rationality). When these qualifications are given due weight, it is not difficult to see that there is such a tendency toward agreement.[9]

I have also indicated why, although religious reasons are not the only kind that should not be the basis for coercion, they are nonetheless special. One consideration is their major role in the sense of identity of many religious people; another is the high authority they have in the eyes of many of them. If certain non-religious reasons can be special in all the ways important for the ethics of citizenship—a contingent matter that cannot be explored here—the principle of secular rationale may be extended to apply to them too. We can imagine, for instance, a mystic who takes apparent readings of tea leaves or a crystal ball to provide reasons for action. Supposing that such a person has a kind of religious devotion to these readings, the reasons might figure in that person's psychology as, for other people, reasons derived from religious experience might. Since some mystical deliverances could yield reasons that are special in the way that religious ones are, the principle of secular rationale could be quite reasonably extended to apply to them, and they would in any case not satisfy its adequacy requirement.

Regarding the exclusivism charge, I have explained why the adequacy requirement does not rule out an important role for religious reasons. The principle of secular rationale allows that religious reasons can be *motivationally* sufficient for properly supporting coercive conduct (this is consistent with adequate secular reasons also being motivationally sufficient). Religious reasons can even be evidentially sufficient to justify the position in question, even though they should not be the sole justification one has. Indeed, it is in part to allow for their adequacy that I do not put all the weight of justifying coercion on the adequacy condition alone. For reasons of the kind brought out in this book, even if we simply required evidentially adequate reasons as justification of coercion, we would still need to distinguish religious considerations from other kinds to formulate a sound ethics of citizenship. In matters of lawmaking, democratic adequacy is more than evidential adequacy.

The Religious, the Secular, and the Spiritual

Defining religion is another problem for understanding secular reasons, as it is for understanding secularity in general. Fortunately, we do not need a definition, as opposed to important criteria for constituting a religion. Here are nine. In calling them *criteria*, I am here implying that each is conceptually relevant to, though not strictly necessary for, a social institution's constituting a religion or (as applied to individuals) to an individual's having a religion: (1) appropriately internalized belief in one or more supernatural beings (gods); (2) observance of a distinction between sacred and profane objects; (3) ritual acts focused on those objects; (4) a moral code believed to be sanctioned by the god(s); (5) religious feelings (awe, mystery, etc.) that tend to be aroused by the sacred objects and during rituals; (6) prayer and other communicative forms concerning the god(s); (7) a worldview according the individual a significant place in the universe; (8) a more or less comprehensive organization of life based on the worldview; and (9) a social organization bound together by (1)–(8).[10]

This characterization is very broad, but that may be desirable. It is better to risk too broad a conception of religion than to err on the side of excessive restriction. To be sure, there are dangers of excessive definatory breadth. One might overextend privileges that may burden society in certain ways, such as tax exemptions for churches and legal permissions to use certain drugs in religious rituals. Definatory breadth, however, tends to be preferable for a free society, and certainly for a liberal democracy, over an unduly narrow conception of religion, since that breadth means protecting liberty and equality better than would be likely on too narrow a conception.

Two further clarifications are needed here. First, on these criteria, a person can be religious without belonging to an institutional religion. Second, secularity is no easier to characterize than religion and has similar vagueness. It is clarifying, however, to note that secularity in individuals is compatible with their being *spiritual*, for instance sensitive to what lies beyond appearances, temperamentally meditative, and not "materialistic" in their pursuits and values. Spirituality, then, is compatible not only with being non-religious but with *secularism*, in the sense of a position calling for a strong separation of church and state and implying opposition to religious worldviews as, for instance, not rational or politically divisive.[11] Secularity in a person is thus compatible with, but does not entail, secularism. Endorsing the principle of secular rationale does not commit one to either of these.

Democratic Adequacy versus Majoritarian Acceptability

Reasons can be adequate to support coercive laws or public policies even if they are not in fact shared by most or all citizens. But one might think that even if adequacy of reasons for such support does not require majoritarian acceptance, the latter—when sincere and freely given—implies the former. An important view that comes close to affirming that implication has been offered by Michael Perry. We "give to others the respect that is their due" as human beings "when we offer them, as explanation, what we take to be our best reasons for acting as we do (so long as our reasons do not assert, presuppose, or entail the inferior humanity of those to whom the explanation is offered)." He continues (objecting to my principle of secular rationale):

According to Robert Audi, "If you are fully rational and I cannot convince you of my view by arguments framed in the concepts we share as rational beings, then even if mine is the majority view I should not coerce you." But *why?* As Gerald Dworkin has observed, "There is a gap between a premise which requires the state to show equal concern and respect for all its citizens and a conclusion which rules out as legitimate grounds for coercion the fact that a majority believes that conduct is immoral, wicked, or wrong." That gap has yet to be closed.[12]

Several points are needed here.

First, Dworkin is speaking of what *governments* may ethically do, and his claim bears mainly on the institutional issue of separation of church and state. I have not claimed that democratic governments may never coerce on the majoritarian basis Dworkin mentions. In some cases, that a majority favors a policy is adequate secular reason to support it (though a majority of the population could be misguided in a way that calls for government's resisting its will so far as possible); nor does his statement even mention whether religious considerations underlie the kind of majority ethical view he cites—much conduct may be considered "immoral, wicked, or wrong" for non-religious reasons. I have already stressed that the autonomy of ethics, which implies that having moral reasons does not entail having religious ones and that moral reasons can be both secular and, as illustrated by a plausible interpretation of the harm principle, adequate for coercion.

Second, Dworkin's claim is consistent with legislators and other officials *as individuals* adhering to (and being obligated to adhere to) the secular rationale principle. If they do, and if they believe that the majority's view is not adequately supported by secular reasons, they may try to change that view or even refuse to support it should that attempt fail. Here courts have a special role, and judges, even more than legislators, may properly take themselves to need adequate secular reason for supporting coercion.

Given these points, the quotation from Dworkin does not express any direct objection to the principle of secular rationale. Perry himself, however, apparently holds what might be called *the respectful sincerity view* (also held by Wolterstorff and others), on which ethics allows voting on any conscientiously chosen basis provided one is sincere and appropriately open about one's reasons and is sufficiently respectful in giving them to fellow citizens.[13] I grant that there is a moral right to act according to the view (if within certain limits); but I contend that the ethics of citizenship requires more of us, including fulfillment of the prima facie obligation expressed in the principle of secular rationale.

Moreover, I do *not* make the case for the secular rationale principle mainly on the basis of requirements for respect or sincerity. The main grounds concern the special conditions under which we may coerce others. These are conditions for limiting freedom, to which there is a very strong right—a right of a kind and strength that justify the ethical limitations on democratic authority indicated by that principle. Not all unjustified restrictions of liberty bespeak any lack of respect. Indeed, respect for people can partly motivate coercion by certain zealots who would save them from error, and it can incline other well-meaning citizens to try to force people to live within respectable limits.

Democracy provides for majoritarian conditions under which liberty rights may be abridged; but a *sound* democracy will not abide by standards that allow government to restrict liberty without reasons that do not depend on religious grounds, and no democracy can be expected to *flourish* unless individuals seek to constrain their own attempts to restrict liberty by adhering to the kinds of standards I have argued for.[14] It is plain that religious people have no difficulty seeing that they would want people in different religions to adhere to these standards; the widely recognized desirability of that kind of reciprocity confirms the soundness of my case. Other elements in that overall case will be introduced shortly.

IV. Natural Reason, Secularity, and Religious Conviction

Some of what has been said bears on the basis of the principle of secular rationale. Regarding the basis of the principle, I will suggest only this. First, it supports democracy and religious liberty, in ways that have been suggested and in still others that will emerge. Second, it helps to prevent religious strife, since it limits coercion to kinds justified on grounds acceptable to any adequately informed, fully rational citizen. Third, adherence to it is needed to achieve the reciprocity among citizens that is required by any plausible understanding of "Do unto others as you would have them do unto you"—which, properly interpreted, is morally compelling and epistemically independent of religion and theology. Rational citizens may properly resent coercion based essentially on someone *else's* religious convictions; adequate secular reasons are not objectionable on that ground.

These considerations parallel those that support separation of church and state at the institutional level. A major support for such separation is the idea that citizens should not be subject to coercion, whether through laws or through public policies, unless it is justifiable by reasons that can be understood and appreciated by fully rational, adequately informed adults independently of their religious position. I have so far stressed, as necessary for justified governmental coercion, "adequate secular reason"—a kind of religiously neutral reason—and I have sought to explicate both secularity and, to some extent, adequacy.[15] But it is important to see that the principle of secular rationale could with virtually equal appropriateness be called *the principle of natural reason*. Almost all who write on religion and politics presuppose a right to religious liberty, and one of my aims here is to connect my theory of the proper relation between government and religion with a conception of the moral rights of citizens. We are witnessing continuing and often sharp controversy over the proper grounds and extent of separation of church and state and, no less important, over the related question of the appropriate balance, in individual political conduct, between religious and political considerations. Let us explore how introducing the notion of natural reason into this controversy may add clarity and reduce polarization.

Natural Reason as Evidentially Secular

By way of background, it should be noted that, as the past two decades have repeatedly shown, the term "secular reason" has been misleading: perhaps owing to its association with *secularism* understood as an orientation opposed to religion and, especially, to religious influences in sociopolitical life, the term has, for many people, suggested a negative attitude toward both. No such attitude is justified by my use of the notion of a secular reason. My account of the notion is purely epistemic: secular reasons are simply *evidentially* independent of religion in a certain way. They do not evidentially depend on the existence of God, or on theological considerations, or on any religious authority. This characterization is theologically neutral and in no way atheistic. Calling for reasons that do not evidentially *depend* on religious considerations in no way implies that no such considerations are evidentially adequate.

It is also important from the perspective of political philosophy that my view is accommodationist in another way as well. It allows (as noted earlier) for the possibility that *religious* reasons bearing on political life can be *both* evidentially adequate and, from an ethical point of view, permissible or even desirable as *motivating* grounds for action. The view also allows that the content of a secular reason—for instance of the idea that a policy will protect religious liberty—can embody the *concept* of religion. The secular, in this epistemic sense, then, is non-religious but not anti-religious. What it precludes is a kind of evidential dependence of the reasons in question. It does not require any particular position on the epistemic status of religious reasons, such as those deriving from scripture, clerical authority, or religious experience.

In part, in speaking of secular reasons as roughly equivalent to natural reasons, I am suggesting that a wider, more ecumenical approach to the relation between religion and politics may be achieved if, in place of the notion of adequate secular reason, we either substitute the notion of adequate natural reason, conceived as a basis for affirming natural rights, or at least supplement and clarify the use of the former by appeal to the latter. This would highlight my central stress on our natural rational endowment and the continuity of my view with certain elements in the natural law tradition as expressed in Aquinas and various later writers. It would also indicate that the principle centers on what rational persons have in common and is not anti-religious.

Clearly we can take our natural endowment as God-given even if we regard the *knowledge* that it makes possible—notably including moral knowledge—as attainable even without dependence on theology or religion. A religion or a theology can make moral claims and even "scientific" (factual) claims—understood roughly as claims having moral or scientific content and confirmable by moral or scientific methods. But there is no good ground for holding either that such claims must be tied to the religion or theology in question for their intelligibility or their justification, or that a religion or theology's implying unreasonable positions in these moral or scientific matters has no bearing on assessing it, particularly in its bearing on sociopolitical life.

Natural Reason as a Normal Human Capacity

More must be said here about natural reason. I refer to a general human capacity for apprehending and responding to grounds for belief and for action. Philosophers usefully speak of human reason in relation to both the theoretical realm, in which we must regulate belief, and the practical realm, in which we must regulate action (practice, in a broad sense). Natural reason is possessed mainly in virtue of the possessors' meeting two everyday standards. One is *theoretical rationality*—the kind exhibited by competent investigation of everyday facts and present when there is an appropriate responsiveness to the grounds for belief. These grounds may be broadly conceived as truth-indicators. The other standard is *practical rationality*—the kind exhibited by competent purposive behavior and present when there is an appropriate responsiveness to grounds for action. Those grounds may be broadly conceived as goodness-indicators. A person who is rational in an overall way—globally rational—must have both kinds of rationality and a significant degree of integration between them.

On the side of theoretical reason, we must include not only responsiveness to sensory experience, memory, and introspective consciousness—for instance a consonance between perceptual experiences and observational beliefs—but also minimal capacities in logic, inductive as well as deductive, and some minimal intuitive capacities. The latter are manifested at least in understanding self-evident propositions. Those include certain propositions in the domain of practical reason, say that if grasping a smoking-hot skillet will cause us excruciating pain, then we have reason not to do this. This is not the place to summarize my overall theory of rationality (developed elsewhere), but what has been said should help to clarify the basic conception of natural reason. It should also help to note a similarity to the view of Aquinas, which is reflected in Descartes and other historically important figures.[16]

A common presupposition of appeals to natural reason is normative authority: natural reason is a capacity for apprehending *genuine* reasons for action or belief, and any consideration that is merely a motivational reason (such as a reason of malice), or only an ostensibly normative one, is not properly called *a* natural reason. Thus, a *merely* secular reason—which is not the kind that concerns this book—need not be a natural one, on the assumption that no consideration merits the term "natural reason" unless it has some minimal normative force.[17]

Might there, however, be a reason that is both secular *and* adequate to support what it is supposed to support, yet not natural? Imagine a technical reason understandable only by highly trained chemists, for instance that having chemical constitution c is a reason to consider a factory's effluent toxic. This is not apprehensible by (unaided) natural reason even supplemented by common-sense knowledge.[18] Still, *that* a highly reliable chemist has testified that a chemical is toxic *is* a natural reason to think it toxic. For the point that a person is reliable on certain topics can be known or evidenced by natural reason, and that such a person's testimony is a reason to believe the person's attestation is also thus apprehensible. Once again, however, it should be stressed that the notion of the natural that I am employing is epistemic, not ontic. Such reasons are not epistemically dependent on religious experience, religious authority, or revelation, but this does not imply that we could apprehend them without divine creation or concurrence. (Think of St. Anselm's appeal to pure reason in his famous ontological argument and Descartes's appeal to the guiding "light of nature" in his *Meditations*.)

Natural reason is plausibly considered an endowment of normal adults who have the kind of understanding of a natural language appropriate to functioning in civil society. This construal rules out cases of deficient mental function of the kind caused by severe handicaps, and there are of course degrees of rational capacity even among people who function quite well in civil society. One reason to raise the question of universality is that we should know just how burdensome a principle of the ethics of citizenship is for those it is supposed to govern. From this point of view it is useful to focus on the minimal level of functioning required by any complex human activity, particularly including religious practice. Given this level, I believe the prima facie obligation to have natural reasons is not in general unfulfillable by religious people and by and large is fulfillable without a heavy burden. Certainly normal adults who are literate enough to understand even the narrative passages in the Bible can get at least a foothold in understanding natural reasons and in seeing some of the benefits of having them where instituting coercive laws or public policies is in question.

Natural Reason and the Status of "Civil Religion"

At this point we should consider an objection that goes beyond pragmatic considerations. Suppose natural reason could take us from ordinary facts, hence naturally (and secularly) knowable premises, to knowledge *both* of God's existence and of specific principles of conduct that God would have us all obey. These might include an obligation to abstain from assisted suicide and abortion, perhaps even a more specific obligation to criminalize those acts. One would think that such premises might at least justify governmental practices exhibiting "civil religion"—such practices as opening legislative sessions with non-denominational prayers—even if not any official establishment of any religion.

Civil religion, in the United States at least, is roughly the national practice of putting God's existence forward in the positive way represented by requiring public school children to recite the Pledge of Allegiance to the Flag of the United States, in which God's sovereignty is implicitly affirmed,[19] by placing "In God We Trust" on U.S. currency, and by often making approving if vague references, in political speeches by government officials and candidates for public office, to God's sovereignty. Unlike institutionalized religion, civil religion has no scripture or creed and is rarely affirmed except by stating or implying one or two tenets at a time. Here I have several points.

First, it is noteworthy that the best theistic arguments from natural theology conclude with the proposition that God exists, not with any specific moral or political directives. Aquinas himself—author of five famous arguments for the existence of God—said:

> [T]he human intellect is not able to reach a comprehension of divine substance through its natural power . . . Yet, beginning with sensible things, our intellect is led to the point of knowing about God that He exists, and other such characteristics that must be attributed to the first Principle.[20]

Those characteristics are quite generic and apparently nonmoral. To be sure, we may assume God is perfectly good; but perfect goodness, by comparison with, say, omnipotence (being all-powerful) and, especially, "creatorship" seems less well supported by the premises of the most plausible theistic arguments provided by natural theology.

Suppose, however, that God's perfect goodness is well supported by natural reason (and that the problem of evil does not threaten the ascription of perfect goodness any more than the other divine attributes). Still, to derive specific moral and political standards from the abstract idea of divine perfect goodness, would we not need a particular theology (e.g. that of a given religion or even denomination), or clerical authority, or religious tradition, or even religious experience—none of which is an element in natural reason? It certainly seems so— and even within a given religious tradition, disagreements about just what God requires of us abound. Given divine perfect goodness alone, no moral standards are derivable from the bare affirmation of God's existence. It does not follow, for instance, that God issues any commands or otherwise communicates specific moral standards to humanity.

Even adding that God creates us *able* to discern moral truths does not entail that God commands obeying any particular ones. If so, then natural reason will not go beyond (epistemically) secular reason in revealing to us substantive ethical directives. Using natural reason alone, to discern what God would have us do we would depend on what we thereby find is morally obligatory. Since, for instance, murder and rape are wrong, we may infer that a supremely good deity would want us to condemn them. The point is not that there is any special limitation in what moral truths may be discoverable through natural theology as including secular moral reasoning, but rather that there would be an apparent equivalence in scope between the moral directives discoverable by natural reason as applied in natural theology and those discoverable using it in a secular way.

My second point here, then, is that if natural reason yields as much normative truth as its proponents have tended to think, then normative truths, or an associated conception of human nature, can be an indication of how God would wish us to behave. This holds, at least, on the assumption that as all-knowing and perfectly good, God would wish us to live in accordance with sound moral standards. Knowledge of them, then, implies truths about divine preference, just as knowledge of laws of nature might reveal aspects of God's plan for the structure of the physical universe.

Here one might appeal to the integration of natural reason with natural law theory as a basis of common morality and legal principles. But suppose that natural law theory is epistemically independent of theology and of one's religious views. Then its playing this role does not differentiate it, in relation to dependence on theology or religion, from rational intuition or other cognitive sources of moral knowledge, such as those appealed to by Kantians or Aristotelians. After all, given God's omniscience and perfect goodness, *any* reliable route to moral truth is in effect a possible route to knowledge of God's wishes for us, since God, as perfectly good, may be taken to wish us to abide by sound moral standards and, as omniscient, must know all moral truths. If, on the other hand, natural law theory is not epistemically independent of theology and religion, then the original problem of determining, by natural reason, divine will for specific dimensions of human conduct remains with us.[21]

A third general point emerges if we consider natural reason a divine gift. Why would this not confer on it, at least in the eyes of theists who take God as all-knowing, all-powerful, and perfectly good, the ability to play a central role both in (1) interpreting theology, religious experience, scripture, and clerical pronouncements, and (2) yielding sociopolitical directives apart from those three sources? Does natural reason not play that role in any case? Consider interpreting scripture. Do we not, for instance, prefer some Biblical interpretations over others because they are more coherent with other parts of the text, where coherence is a standard central for natural reason? And do we not question the genuineness of a religious experience if it seems to support a belief that goes against what is eminently reasonable in the sense appropriate to natural reason?

Ambiguity between the Ethical and the Theological

This is a good place to note cases in which important terms are used in such a way that their force is, for some, theological, if only in the thin sense implicit in civil religion and, for others, a matter of what is justified through natural reason. Consider the idea that

> [t]he proposition that all human beings are sacred is, for many persons, a religiously based tenet . . . The proposition is an axiom of many secular moralities as well . . . As Ronald

> Dworkin has written, "We almost all accept . . . that human
> life in all its forms is *sacred*. . . . For some of us, this is a matter
> of religious faith; for others, of secular but deep philosoph-
> ical belief."[22]

One would normally think that the sacred is something deserving reverence because of its relation to God or at least to
religion. If so, then appealing to the sacredness of human beings to justify actions, laws, or policies implies according normative authority to God or some religious person, scripture, or
tradition. Such appeals may be offensive, evasive, or otherwise
unacceptable to secular citizens or indeed to religious ones who
do not agree on the claimed sacredness. *Anyone* who disagrees
on the conclusion supported by a sacredness claim may find the
claim unacceptably dogmatic if unexplained and objection-
ably sectarian if given a theological or religious explanation
or grounding.

Suppose, on the other hand, that the sacred is the "inviolable" or simply something otherwise rights-protected. Would
it not be at least more ecumenical and clearer to use terms of
that kind and explain them by appeal to such natural reasons
as the right to, or value of, liberty, free expression, education,
or protections from injury? Appeals to such considerations
may be guided by one's theology and even motivated by one's
sense that these religious sources demand respecting the
values in question. The point is that in supporting coercion,
having adequate considerations of these secular kinds and offering them in appropriate ways is prima facie obligatory and
needed for the optimal function of a pluralistic democracy.

Here and in relation to other points in this chapter, some
theists might reason as follows. Even if we rely on natural reason to show us the way to God intellectually, once we find Him
we may throw away the ladder and direct our lives by divine
will. This move, however, is open to competing theistic worldviews, and it can lead to irreconcilable disagreements between

their votaries as to what God requires of us. These disagreements can be virulent. There may be no way on earth to make peace so long as people oppose one another under the banners of their clashing religious doctrines. For these and other reasons, a democracy should not endorse (though it should also not legally prohibit) appeals to reasons drawn from such bases in determining one's support of coercive laws or public policies. This point does not imply, however, that religious considerations of the kind in question can have no sociopolitical role or must be "privatized" in democratic politics. The principle of secular rationale constrains but does not eliminate their role, nor does it license coercion of a kind that would abrogate the rights of conscience. It provides for religious reasons to have a major role in justification, motivation, self-expression, and even political discourse.

V. Religious Reasons, Political Decision, and Toleration

In the light of what has been said here, we can address a challenge to the principle of secular rationale presented in a wide-ranging paper by Habermas that addresses religion and democracy. Habermas maintains that the "demand [of the secular rationale principle] is countered by the objection that many religious citizens would not be able to undertake such an artificial division within their own minds without jeopardizing their existence as pious persons . . . A devout person pursues her daily rounds by *drawing* on belief."[23] Call this *the artificial division objection.*

To appraise this objection, consider two elements in the passage: the suggestion that the distinction between the religious and the secular is artificial and the idea that, for many religious citizens, making it would jeopardize their identity. Regarding the first, without denying that there are borderline cases, surely there are many clear ones. It should help to think in terms of natural rather than secular reasons: the relevant natural reasons are all secular in the epistemic sense. Public health rationales for inoculations are clearly secular; the view that duty to God requires opening school days with prayer is clearly religious. Requiring inclusion of evolutionary biology in high school science on the ground that it is considered scientifically central by the vast majority of biological scientists is an appeal to a secular rationale.

By contrast, *some* rationales for requiring that creationism be included in teaching biology are clearly not secular, for instance the premise that respect for God's sovereignty requires endorsingly teaching the Genesis account of creation. I grant that a case can be made for the secularity of the contention that intellectual responsibility and respect for religious perspectives requires, in such a science curriculum, *recognizing* creationism (or at least intelligent design) as possible accounts of the origin of the human species. This contention, to be sure, involves the *concept* of religion, but it makes no appeal to any religious truth or authority. The notion of a natural reason, even that of a secular one, does not preclude religious concepts from figuring in their *content*; these notions are epistemically, not contentually, independent of religion and theology. Once we take into account the grounds as opposed to the content of statements offered as reasons for laws or public policies and at the same time orient discussion around clear cases, we can see that the distinction between the religious and the secular and, correspondingly, between religious and natural reasons, is clear enough to do the kinds of important work in political philosophy that are needed for the purposes of this book.

In the light of these examples, we can also address the jeopardized identity idea. Why would distinguishing between religious and natural reasons threaten a devout person's identity? The principle of secular rationale does not imply that religious reasons are not *good*, nor even that secular ones are more truth-conducive. It is also proposed with the specific understanding that religious people can *view* the former as generally better reasons and can be motivated more (or wholly) by them. The principle posits a prima facie obligation to have adequate secular reasons for supporting institutional coercion; it does not preclude or disparage religious reasons.

It may help here to consider the power of the Golden Rule: any normal adult can understand, on the basis of natural reason, the revulsion to being compelled to do something, say to kneel and recite imprecatory prayers, on the basis of some-one *else's* religious convictions. If we can rationally want others to abstain from coercing us on the basis of their religious reasons, we can understand religious reasons well enough to be guided by the principle of secular rationale. In the very under-standing of one's own religious view and how it differs from others, one has much of what is needed to distinguish religious reasons from other kinds and to see some of the grounds for our obligation to have adequate secular reasons as a basis for coercive laws or public policies.

It is interesting to note that Habermas himself suggests that "religious citizens must develop an epistemic stance toward the priority that secular reasons enjoy in the political arena."[24] In my view, this injunction presupposes the concep-tual abilities needed for the principle of secular rationale. One could not reliably follow it without being able to identify secular reasons and to compare them with other kinds. Haber-mas's view is thus a quite inadequate basis to sustain his criti-cism of mine.

A further point emerges if we assume what Habermas calls a "requirement of [secular] translation": "The truth content of religious contributions can only enter into the institutional practice of deliberation and decision-making if the necessary translation [of "convictions in a religious language"] already occurs in . . . the political public sphere itself" (p. 10). This requirement implies not only that educated religious citizens can *understand* secular as well as religious discourse but also that they can find an appropriately strong *correspondence* between the two realms.[25] The second implication, then—the correspondence demand that (at least by implication) Habermas makes on religious citizens—is stronger than any implication of the principle of secular rationale, which (among other things) does not entail that such correspondence can always be found. Both points, however, support the conclusion that the suggestion of the principle of secular rationale's jeopardizing identity is unwarranted.

A Political Role of Religious Reasons

I have explained how the principle of secular rationale—of natural reason, we might also say—leaves open not only that religious reasons can be aligned with secular ones and can be a cogent basis for action, but that they can, like secular reasons, constrain those who seek to restrict liberty. Let me, then, stress a principle that indicates a sociopolitical role for religious reasons and constitutes a complementary companion to the secular rationale principle:

> *The principle of religious rationale.* Religious citizens in a democratic society have a prima facie obligation not to advocate or support any law or public policy that restricts human conduct, unless they have, and are willing to offer, adequate religious reason for this advocacy or support.

The underlying idea is that the ethics of good citizenship calls on religious citizens to constrain their coercion of fellow citizens by seeking a rationale from their own religious perspective—a rationale that is both religious in content and genuinely justificatory.[26] This is a perspective that, in such a weighty matter, it would be hypocritical or worse for a religious citizen to ignore, especially (though not only) where coercion is in question. That point is defensible both on ethical grounds and from at least the majority of religious perspectives— including some from which the principle of secular rationale would be rejected. This point is one reason why the religious rationale principle may be considered an element in the ethics of citizenship for religious citizens.

Moreover, given the common coincidence in implication between religious reasons for legal constraints on freedom and natural reasons (which would also be secular reasons) for the same constraints, the principle of religious rationale is an important complement to its secular counterpart. The same kind of coincidence might be expected regarding religious and secular reasons for supporting basic liberties. Both kinds of reasons support the freedom to practice religion and the freedom to be spared having to do so at the behest of someone else. Nor is freedom of religion the only central case; the dignity of persons, which is supportable on both religious and secular grounds, is another basis of convergence between religious and secular reasons.

The principle of religious rationale is important for at least three further reasons. It draws attention to the importance of seeking adequate reasons before instituting or supporting coercive laws or public policies. It also indicates a respect for religious reasons as worthy of consideration and potentially justificatory. Third, it serves as a reminder that the religious reasons of some may conflict with those of others. This, in the context of the "Do-unto-others" principle, tends to leaven the zeal that can fuel coercion.

VI. Privatization versus Activism: The Place of Religious Considerations in Public Political Discourse

I have distinguished standards for ethically justifiable advocacy from standards for ethically justifiable free expression, and I have suggested that, in ways my principles indicate, the ethics of citizenship places stronger constraints on the former than on the latter. Let me conclude this chapter with some points concerning some of the standards for religious expression—whether argumentative or simply expressive—in public discourse. So far as religion is concerned (and I continue to focus on the relation between religion and politics), these standards are in effect standards for *non*-privatization of religion.

Religious Discourse in Politics and Government

We might begin with the point that the uses of religious language are unlimited: think not just of advocacy and persuasion, but of self-expression, self-description, and providing information that may inform discussion. I may need to tell you my religious position to say, in any depth, who I am. I might also want to *persuade* an audience of religious physicians or attorneys not to violate our relation to God by facilitating assisted suicide; and I might make this religious case even though I have, and say that I have, *voted* to legalize it, for natural reasons based on respect for the liberty of others with different religions or none. Sometimes, quite apart from the degree of cogency of the case we make, we are more persuasive with those who can identify with us—or simply feel they know us—than we would otherwise be. Achieving persuasion might be facilitated by bringing appropriate religious considerations into one's discourse.

The position I have been presenting is in sharp contrast with Judge Michael McConnell's view that "the 'principle of secular rationale' rests on a false distinction between generally accessible reasons and religious ideas . . . and that there is no convincing constitutional or philosophical reason that democratic deliberation should be secular."[27] Let me take the separable points here in turn.

First, I make no claim that all religious ideas are inaccessible, on the basis of natural reason, to normal adult citizens. Indeed, some of these ideas correspond to ethical principles understood from the point of view of natural reason. But religious experience or sheer religious authority may, in the thinking of some people, figure as grounds of reasons, and in this case we either do not have accessible grounds in a relevant sense or do not have a basis in natural reason for either belief or action. One cannot expect to have religious experiences substantially like those of others and may not even understand what those experiences are like. Moreover, one person's absolute religious truth may be another person's abominable heresy.

Second, a reason can figure importantly in deliberation even if it is restricted in the moderate way that the principle of secular rationale requires. This principle does not preclude even overtly religious reasons from playing a role—evidential as well as clarificatory, persuasive, and motivational—in such deliberation. Its force is instead to constrain that role in a way that is defensible from many religious perspectives as well as from a secular point of view.

A third point is that the constraints appropriate to the discourse and deliberations of the judiciary and, perhaps to a lesser extent, to legislators and others in government acting officially, are stronger than those appropriate to citizens as such. Judges should represent, at least implicitly, not only the citizenry but also the constitution or other basic legal structure under which they are sworn to work. Legislators are representatives of their constituents, and in a sound democracy this implies respecting secular as well as religious citizens—or, if there should be no secular ones—protecting the religious liberty to move from a religious to a secular outlook (a basic right noted in the Universal Declaration of Human Rights and elsewhere).

The difficulties determining what constitutes proper democratic representation deserve more discussion than they can receive here, but enough has been said to indicate that there are differences in the degree to which different categories of citizens are obligated to observe the principle of secular rationale. I suggest that any plausible theory of representation in democratic government will also indicate that democratic authority is limited by that principle as well as by the liberty, equality, and neutrality principles.

Given these points, there is no justification for speaking of epistemic "pre-screening devices like the principle of secular rationale."[28] Religious reasons are not implied to be inadmissible in political discourse, inappropriate as possible evidences, or epistemically deficient. Still, by themselves, they should not be taken to justify coercion by law or public policy in democratic societies. There are many reasons for this, but the point is most easily seen to be plausible in the light of reflection on the Do-unto-others principle.

Lifting Oppression as a Special Case

A further point is needed to indicate another reason why McConnell's critical remarks do not undermine the principle of secular rationale. In criticizing Rawls's view (and by implication mine) he says, "Abolitionists and civil rights leaders . . . advanced religious arguments to bring about a more just society, and they defined justice by reference to their own religious convictions."[29] I have stressed that the principle of secular rationale applies to coercion, not liberalizations.[30] Indeed, I have also indicated that the prima facie obligation it posits can be overridden if religious considerations are the only kind motivationally strong enough to prevent the rise of a tyrant. A prima facie reason can be strong and should not be ignored even when overridden. But it can be overridden.

One reason why liberalization, as lifting restrictions of freedom, differs from coercion in the range of reasons appropriate to supporting it is that freedom is the default position in liberal democracy and may properly be supported by a wider variety of reasons than those needed to justify coercion. Coercion of adult citizens must be justified by such natural reasons as that permitting certain liberties would be harmful to persons; liberalization can be justified by simply showing the lack of adequate natural reasons for coercion, and, arguably, may be properly supported by conscientiously held personal reasons that, in a liberal democracy, include religious ones. Other things equal, democracies should seek not only to permit but also to protect the freedoms of action and expression that citizens normally show a deep and enduring desire to have.

None of this implies that appeal to religious reasons favoring liberalization is always evidentially adequate or otherwise desirable; it may be not only unneeded but intellectually weak, misleading, or even divisive. Still, where religious reasons for liberalization, say for lifting oppression, are combined with secular ones, this may have the good effect of enhancing both justification and motivation to act accordingly and of indicating an important case in which the two kinds of reasons coincide in their implications for law or public policy.

The admissibility of religious considerations in certain cases of supporting liberalization is one thing; its desirability is quite another. Even where we seek to enhance liberty, we can still be injudicious in the *way* we appeal to religious considerations, even where doing so is in itself unobjectionable or even desirable. Doing it in a sectarian way, as where we appeal to a controversial clerical authority or a disputed reading of scripture, may invite those with competing religious views to enter the discussion in such a way that avoidable trouble and perhaps serious strife will ensue. To be sure, there are apparently "comprehensive reasons" (in Rawls's sense), such as the value of a Kantian kind of autonomy in human life, that are shared by all the religious traditions likely to be represented in a political discussion in a democracy. But, even where such commonality among religions exists, noting it may or may not lead to people's bringing into public discourse religious arguments that unify rather than divide them.[31]

Churches as Institutional Citizens

The points so far made are addressed to individual citizens but also bear on the conduct of religious institutions and indeed on that of clergy acting as such and not simply as citizens. This is an important dimension of the topic of the proper relation between religion and politics. Church-state separation is often conceived unidirectionally. But separation is symmetrical. This leads me to propose two principles as desirable guides for clergy.

The first guiding principle is

> *The principle of ecclesiastical political neutrality:* Churches committed to being institutional citizens in democracy have a prima facie obligation to abstain from supporting candidates for public office or pressing for laws or public policies that restrict human conduct, particularly religious or other basic liberties.[32]

This principle applies not only to religious institutions as social entities but (where this is different) to their official representatives acting as such. Even for churches not committed to institutional citizenship, a case can be made that their accepting such a prima facie obligation of neutrality would be good. For one thing, it would tend to support their commitment to their own religious mission. Political involvement is often highly preoccupying, and competent political action requires time and energy that could instead be devoted to the internal needs of the church and its members. Moreover, their accepting such a principle would also tend to conduce to political stability insofar as that is threatened by competition among religious institutions in the political arena. Admittedly, we already live with some tensions of this sort, and their effects need not all be bad; but they would be much worse than they are if there were not a great many churches generally inclined to follow something like the ecclesiastical political neutrality principle voluntarily.

It might be thought that if churches give adequate secular reason for any political conduct of the kind that the principle of ecclesiastical neutrality concerns, this would suffice for their properly engaging in that conduct. But this view would miss two important points. First, this is a church-state separation principle and cannot play its proper role even with that qualification. Indeed, note that the same might be said of the separation principles restricting government in relation to religion—those of liberty, equality, and neutrality. These do not allow governmental restrictions on religious conduct simply for adequate secular reasons: only a subset of those can suffice, mainly weighty considerations of protection of the populace from harm or discrimination against a particular religion or against citizens or institutions. The second point is that the ecclesiastical neutrality principle is justified from the point of view of *institutional ethics*: the role of churches— a role partly responsible for their special place in pluralistic democracies—tends to be compromised by political activity of the kind in question.

It might also be thought that if churches are willing to give up their tax-exempt status, they then have a perfect right to be politically active. That may be true. My point is not that they do not have such a right—much as do labor unions and professional organizations. The point is that this right is one that there is a prima facie obligation not to exercise. Civic virtue can exist at the institutional level. Churches, perhaps more than any other kind of institution, should practice it. They realize it best when they abide by the principle of ecclesiastical political neutrality.

The Ethical Responsibilities of Clergy

A second principle is suggested by the point that ideals of civic virtue apply to clergy as individuals as well as to churches as institutions. In my view, even in making avowedly personal statements clergy who believe in freedom and democracy should follow an individual neutrality principle that complements the institutional principle of ecclesiastical political neutrality, which concerns their conduct as church representatives. Its individual counterpart is

> *The principle of clerical political neutrality*: Clergy have a prima facie obligation to observe a distinction between their personal political views and their views *as* clergy, to prevent any political aims they may have from dominating their professional conduct, and to abstain from officially (as church leaders) supporting candidates for public office or pressing for laws or policies that would restrict human conduct.

This principle is in no tension with clergy as individuals following the principles of religious and secular rationale—with all the freedom to use religious reasons they provide for. Nor need the former principle conflict with the point that applying religious principles and insights to issues of law and public policy can be highly beneficial. Nonetheless, it is appropriate that clergy exercise restraint in dealing with political issues, particularly in public. If they do not, they may not only fall short in their central commitment to religious leadership; they may also invite peers who disagree to use religious leverage for opposite ends, and the public, quite possibly including their own congregations, may then suffer from inter-religious conflicts. There is a significant risk of inducing political discord in parishes or denominations that might otherwise enjoy a deeper unity.

It may be objected that the proposed neutrality principles are too broad in ruling out churches and clergy taking moral positions that are politically controversial. It is true that the principles depend on the distinction between the moral and the political. But that dependency is intrinsic to any theory of clerical virtue and poses a challenge for any theory of separation of church and state or of the relation between religion and politics. Three points will help. One is that at least numerous moral propositions representing a great many kinds of considerations are secular in the sense in which reasons have been said to be so above. The second point is that if some propositions are both moral and religious, say that it is morally wrong to disobey God's command not to kill, either their behavioral directive (in this case, abstention from killing people) can be justified by natural reason or they do not ground cogent objections to the principles.

The third point needed here is negative. A position need not be considered political simply because it is politically controversial, say a focus of contention between opposing political parties. Thus, stem cell research raises moral issues that are politically controversial, but its moral permissibility is not thereby a political question. Suppose that the two neutrality principles permit clergy to take public positions on its morality. It does not follow that those positions may thereby be unobjectionably argued in public wholly on the basis of religious considerations. The principles make advocacy of laws or public policies wholly on this basis prima facie impermissible. They also make it prima facie impermissible, for churches, as for clergy acting officially, to recommend *voting* for or against candidates on the basis of their positions on these issues, even if that basis is not political.

The Political, the Moral and the Religious

Something further should be said about the difference between the moral and the political. It should be evident that the ecclesiastical neutrality principle is misconstrued if 'political' is taken in the sense of 'contested in the arena of politics'"—the *polemical sense*—or in the *philosophical sense*, as in 'political philosophy', where it means roughly 'concerning the appropriate or the basic structure of civil society'. The term 'political' must be taken rather narrowly, so that moral issues are not construed as necessarily political, even if they enter into political debates. But the term must not be taken so narrowly that pressing for restrictive laws or public policies—such as policies requiring recitation of the Pledge of Allegiance in public schools—does not count as political. This holds even if the political action is motivated by moral considerations (though that factor may mitigate certain violations of the separation principles proposed in this book). If moral motivation of an action prevented its qualifying as political, even paradigmatic political acts like speeches promoting a candidate and party would sometimes not qualify.

In the paradigm cases of the narrowly political, the notion of the political essentially concerns *who* among specific people will (or should) govern, for instance who will win an election, or secure an appointment in government, in a political party, or perhaps a university or a large business. A paradigm of a political preference in this sense is favoring a particular candidate for office. To be sure, conduct that is political in the wider, roughly philosophical, sense can be motivated by what is political in the narrow sense (and conversely): that conduct can be a disguised way to gain favor for one's own party or candidate. But the distinction between the political in the narrow sense and the moral remains viable in principle and is important in practice.

This distinction can be masked by the application of a single term, such as 'the abortion issue', to both moral questions about ethical permissibility and political questions about whose policies regarding a kind of behavior should be enacted. (Questions about the exact conditions under which the law should allow it may be either moral or narrowly political or straddle both categories.) Paradigms of political questions in the narrow sense are what specific people or what particular party will or should hold governmental power. Somewhat less clear cases—at least they are not necessarily political in the narrow sense—are what policies should govern relations, including immigration, with specific foreign countries (for here determinate individuals and their rights are directly at stake). We might speak here of what is political in *the social policy sense.*

When we come to what specific structure should be enacted for taxation, welfare, criminal justice, healthcare, and military systems, we have issues that can be treated as political in the broad, philosophical sense, for instance where general criteria in these domains are at issue from the point of view of social justice. But social justice can also be construed as political in a narrower sense, depending on how clearly the adoption of a policy in such domains would give governmental power to specific individuals. There are many other kinds of political questions. Some of these questions have major moral dimensions, and we cannot hope to make a plausible distinction between the moral and the political that is sharp enough to put every sociopolitical question clearly on one side or the other.

It is particularly difficult to determine whether a moral condemnation of something a candidate for office proposes is political in the sense that it implies recommending a vote against the candidate. Much depends on the context. Is the condemnation combined with plausible arguments that might be used to dissuade the candidate? Does it leave room to treat merits of the candidate as outweighing the moral error in question? Might the candidate's objectionable policies be unlikely to be enacted even if the candidate is elected? Are alternative candidates even worse? Is the clerical condemnation accompanied by a threat, say of excommunication (a threat that has in fact been used)? A properly worded moral condemnation that may have political implications is unlikely, without further premises, to entail an endorsement of specific political actions. It may thus be ethically valuable while at the same time operating at a certain inferential distance from the citizen's action at the ballot box.

The separation of church and state does not require, nor do any sound principles demand, that churches should not publicly take moral positions, even if there is political controversy about them. Publicly taking moral positions is indeed both a positive religious obligation in many religions and one whose exercise may be ethically beneficial for pluralistic democracies. There are, to be sure, different ways of supporting moral positions. Some are closer than others to political statements, as where government officials of only one party are cited as immoral despite the prominence of comparable offenders who are officials in another party. Clergy should in general seek to avoid even the appearance of partisanship. These matters call for discretion and do not admit of codification.

So far, I have been making broad points about the conditions under which religious reasons may be brought into public discourse consistently with the principle of secular rationale and the principles of ecclesiastical and clerical neutrality. I have left open some matters of judgment that deserve brief comment before I conclude.

What are some of the general *standards* of good citizenship for the sociopolitical use of religious discourse, including quotations from scripture, descriptions of religious experience, and appeals to clerical authority? One is simply judiciousness. Will what we say be illuminating or alienating, consensus-building or divisive, clarifying or obfuscating? There are myriad considerations here, of both ethical sensitivity and prudence. A second consideration is a spirit of reciprocity, based partly on a sense of universal standards available to all rational, minimally educated adult citizens. An appeal to a Biblical narrative, for instance, can be clarifying with regard to such secular questions as whether prosperous nations are obligated to give more than they do to poor ones. Consider also the "Do-unto-others" rule. The *wording* is Biblical; the *content* is a call for reciprocity, even universalizability. Both are standards that, in some form, are also central in any plausible secular ethics.

It should be clear that I see no conflict between being religious, indeed expressively so, in public, and adhering to both the principle of secular rationale and that of religious rationale. This integration is most likely to be well reasoned and stable if it is supported by a theoethical equilibrium, the kind of rational integration (described in Chapter 1) between religious and religiously grounded deliverances and insights concerning moral matters and, on the other hand, secular ethical considerations. There are theological reasons, at least from the point of view of *natural* theology, for thinking that a high degree of such integration is possible at least for those who, like many religious people, conceive God as all-knowing, all-powerful, and perfectly good. Religious citizens who achieve theoethical equilibrium will typically have *both* natural and religious reasons for their standards governing freedom and coercion.

––––––––

The relation between religion and politics is a topic of great importance in the current global climate. Religion is often a powerful force in politics, a pervasive element in the culture of a nation, and influential in most other realms of human life. In many Western societies where the influence of religion has waned among educated citizens, its influence among immigrants is often growing. In societies where religion has been suppressed, we are seeing changes that are partly responsible for its apparent gain in adherents and influence. Whatever its sociocultural role in one or another society, as we strive to support democratic government we must find a sound and credible theory of the standards that should structure governmental relations toward both institutional religion and religious individuals. I have proposed and defended three principles toward this end: one calling for governmental protection of religious liberty to the fullest extent possible under the harm principle, the second requiring government to treat different religions equally, and the third requiring governmental neutrality toward religion.

Despite the breadth of these standards, they do not address the ethics of citizenship as regards individuals in their sociopolitical conduct. For that case I have defended a principle of secular rationale—of natural reason—aimed at enhancing cooperation in pluralistic societies while recognizing, indeed respecting, the importance of religious perspectives and convictions that, especially where this principle is not followed, may often divide people. This principle should be combined with a counterpart principle of religious rationale, which calls on religious citizens to seek adequate religious reasons before advocating coercive laws or public policies. Both principles are complemented by the principles of ecclesiastical and clerical neutrality.

All of these principles support positing a prima facie obligation to respect liberty and to restrict it only for the kinds of reasons that can be both respected and shared by rational, adequately informed citizens regardless of their religious position. At the same time, the principles make room for religious reasons to shape inquiry, to figure in deliberation, and to guide the discourse of religious citizens when, in the public sphere, they are speaking or, especially, advocating law or policy. The proper role of religious reasons in attempts to justify coercion is limited, but this is, in the long run, as much a protection of religious liberty as of the freedom rights of all citizens irrespective of their religious convictions.

CHAPTER 4

DEMOCRATIC TOLERANCE AND RELIGIOUS OBLIGATION IN A GLOBALIZED WORLD

We live in a world beset by disagreement and strife. As the previous chapters have shown in relation to many segments of civic life, a great deal of the disagreement and strife has a largely religious basis. But many other elements produce tensions and hostilities, and a major challenge for political philosophy is to provide an account of the conditions under which a rational person or a governmental body should tolerate a kind of behavior that seems wrong or otherwise undesirable, rather than coerce or attack its perpetrators. This is a major undertaking, and I approach it mainly in connection with public policy regarding religion. Religion is one of the most important elements that raise the challenge. I proceed against the background of the earlier chapters, which express a general political philosophy that treats liberty and a kind of basic political equality as constitutive standards in any morally sound democratic state. To be sure, the need for working principles to guide governments in relation to religion and religious institutions in relation to government goes beyond democracies. Monarchies still exist; and, even where they have an established church, they too should accommodate religious liberty, and they may be expected to be, if not neutral toward religion, then at least not unjust toward the non-religious or those in minority religions.

The previous chapters formulate not just positive aims for lawmaking and public policy but also constraints on political conduct, both governmental and individual. They indicate necessary conditions for coercion that minimally justify it but do not indicate when its imposition is desirable. But justification by only minimally adequate reasons is compatible with lawmaking or public policy that is at best undesirable. What is minimally justifiable is not blameworthy, but it need not deserve endorsement.

This chapter extends and refines the position so far developed by addressing some problems concerning toleration that remain even when such a wide-ranging position in political philosophy is in place. Abstention from supporting laws or public policies entails a kind of tolerance, but not *every* kind. Where we should not coerce (as in outlawing certain kinds of controversial conduct), we may or may not be tolerant of the behavior in other respects. There are many kinds and degrees of toleration; and even when a kind of conduct is protected by law, it may not be fully tolerated or tolerated in the right way. To see this, we should first explore what constitutes tolerance. The philosophical literature has often discussed its limits, and these are one of my concerns; but understanding it from the point of view of moral psychology is also a challenge.

I. The Nature of Tolerance

Tolerance is compatible with harmonious relations between those who tolerate and those whose conduct they tolerate, but it is clear that tolerance does not entail approval. Indeed, it implies disapproval or at least a kind of dislike. But tolerance is not only—and not mainly—attitudinal; it is also behavioral. To tolerate is in part to abstain from preventive actions, or certain kinds of discouragement, toward the persons, actions, or things one disapproves of. Tolerance is especially important in matters of religion, since religious beliefs so often generate violent disapproval of how outsiders, whether religious or not, conduct their lives.[1]

Behavioral tolerance is not simply a matter of abstaining from interference; that is possible for an indifferent person. It is at least abstaining from certain kinds of interferences despite a negative attitude toward, or at least a kind of dislike of, the conduct in question. One may, to be sure, seek to *persuade* those one tolerates not to do the things one disapproves of, and efforts to persuade need not be interferences. Forbearance from compulsion does not imply abstention from criticism or dissuasion. Those may be highly civilized, even quite friendly; they need not rise to interference, but may do so. That is one reason why *how* we tolerate can be almost as important as *what* we tolerate.

Every agent has some power, but an agent cannot be properly said to tolerate someone or some behavior unless that agent has some power regarding it. This does not imply the power of prevention, but normally does imply the power to impede. The ethics of the use of power is crucial, and it should be no surprise that a theory of democratic tolerance must draw on basic ethical theory. The ethics of tolerance is mainly addressed to the powerful, and particularly to governments; but virtually everyone is in a position to tolerate something, and nearly everyone must do so as a condition of peaceful coexistence with others.

These points should make it clear that tolerance is morally complex. It may be attitudinally criticizable even where it is behaviorally justified. Suppose neighbors play loud music at a Saturday picnic and at a volume that makes it inescapable even indoors. On some such occasions, one ought not to interfere. This would be behavioral tolerance. Such tolerance might still be accompanied by an unduly hostile attitude toward playing the music, and one might, to a third party about to join the picnic, scathingly criticize the neighbors' playing the music. This criticism might be inappropriately harsh and unjustifiably timed. The possibility of such unjustifiable expressions of a negative attitude does not imply that tolerance requires attitudinal neutrality or abstention from efforts to dissuade; but in some cases a quiet forbearance may be best even where what is tolerated is undesirable or even wrong.

Tolerance may, then, be justified both behaviorally and attitudinally, but expressed in ethically inappropriate *ways*. It may be too vocal, too intrusive, too patronizing. It must achieve a mean between the excess of officious zeal and the deficiency of indifference toward the positive changes that would make it unnecessary. Take the case of the treatment of women in certain conservative religious sects. Where it must be tolerated in some cases (though not where it entails human sacrifice or certain physical abuses), there are right and wrong ways to tolerate. Passive disapproval of unequal treatment is criticizably lax; overzealous criticism may infringe both liberty and privacy rights and also be counterproductive.

II. Is Tolerance a Virtue?

The idea that tolerance should achieve a mean between excess and deficiency suggests that, when sufficiently rooted and pervasive in a person to count as a trait of character, it is a virtue. This does not imply that every manifestation of a tolerant nature is virtuous. Even in highly tolerant persons, not every type of tolerant act they perform manifests their virtue; an affectionate whim can produce a tolerant and kind deed. A good case can be made, however, for a kind of tolerance being a virtue, but only if it is understood that tolerance is not a *moral* virtue. A wholly amoral person could be tolerant.

Even people who are not amoral can be tolerant for the wrong kinds of reasons, say by putting up graciously with things they disapprove of and could prevent, but where they tolerate the wrong kinds of things and do not tolerate the kinds of things—such as annoying but morally permissible exercises of free speech—that merit toleration. Their tolerance in this case is not morally sound, nor does it count toward their moral goodness. It seems possible, then, to be tolerant in the characterological sense, yet not have the virtue of tolerance. Even a rooted tendency to put up with things one dislikes need not be virtuous: its manifestations may be unguided by discretion, its dislikes ill-chosen, and its exercises accompanied by unwarranted resentment.

One might, to be sure, say the same of courage or conscientiousness, which are in themselves good traits but (in a way not possible for, say, justice and veracity) can serve not just moral ends but also immoral ones. Tolerance is like them in containing no moral standard within itself. Like them, it might be thought to be an *adjunctive virtue*—adjunctive from the point of view of moral virtue, in the sense that it assists the person in realizing moral virtue but is not itself a moral virtue, such as justice, fidelity, or veracity.[2] Those traits, by contrast, are in part morally constituted. Even if a person possessed just one of these together with major vices, it would be, from the moral point of view, *mitigatory*. An honest dictator could be brutal and morally abhorrent; but there would still be one thing morally good about such a person, and its significance would suffice to prevent being as bad as a dictator otherwise similar but without even that morally good trait.

The Normativity of Tolerance as a Virtue

If tolerance is like courage in being a virtue at all, then even if it is not moral, it is *normative*. Consider courage first. Being courageous requires making sound judgments in situations where different values conflict, say self-protection and, on the other side, furthering a valued cause such as victory in battle. We cannot be courageous just by exhibiting bravery in habitually putting at risk just anything we care about for the sake of something else. It would be folly to risk one's life to save an ordinary snowman one simply happens to like. One might speak of "guts" here, but not courage. Is tolerance similarly governed by rough standards concerning the range of values in question? Mere tolerance is not, but this does not hold for tolerance as a virtue.

If we are thinking of tolerance as a virtue, we will view it in relation to putting up with things that, on the basis of a certain range of values, one disapproves of or dislikes. They need not be moral, but they cannot be just any basis of aversion. A person who abstains from tearing off a companion's hated hat is not thereby exhibiting the virtue of tolerance, even if, given the power to remove it, the abstention would count as an act of toleration. Even a pattern of diverse abstentions of this subjective kind would not imply possessing any virtue. We can distinguish, then, between tolerance as a psychological disposition constituted by a suitably strong tendency to resist aversive impulses and, on the other hand, tolerance as a trait of character that is governed by values of a certain kind. Paradigms of these values are moral ones, and especially prominent are the values of freedom and autonomy. Valuing these is particularly important in political and religious matters. It is, above all, exercises of rights of liberty and self-government that provide the occasion for development and exercises of tolerance as a virtue.

If we can frame a clear account of tolerance as a virtue, do we then have a basic standard for determining the limits of liberty in a morally sound democratic society? In answering, it is crucial to distinguish a necessary condition for a (morally) sound democracy from a basic standard for being a democracy at all. If a society is not, in its legal structure and the behavior of citizens, duly tolerant, it is not a democracy and certainly not a sound democracy. If a society is a democracy at all, free expression at least at the ballot box must be tolerated by those in power. Suppose, however, that the citizens themselves are intolerant. Then, a democracy they dominate could be significantly intolerant—political freedom is required for democracy of any kind, but that freedom is compatible with a high degree of democratically instituted intolerance in matters of lifestyle, art, and religion.

Constitutional versus Procedural Democracy

The possibility of a high level of intolerance in a democratic society is one reason why a sound democracy cannot be characterized purely procedurally, say as one governed by the will of the majority. The errors and vices of a single individual can be multiplied across an entire society, and they can stain the ballot box.[3] In non-constitutional monarchies and other non-democratic forms of government, intolerance would also be a defect (even though it is unlikely that these forms of government can be morally sound at all). We can see, then, that tolerance can be a characteristic of states, governments, and institutions—call this *institutional tolerance.* Individual tolerance is not the only kind.

It is particularly important to distinguish tolerance as a virtue—institutional as well as individual—from the minimal protection of liberty necessary for being a democracy at all. Given that not everything we have a right to do is something we should do, and that some things we have a right to do may even be wrong, a democracy that protects our moral rights must behaviorally tolerate some wrongs. Even a purely procedural democracy must protect the right to vote in free elections. This minimal behavioral tolerance need not manifest institutional virtue. That right might be exercised, and legally protected, for the wrong reasons, indeed for morally objectionable reasons such as simply doing what one's clerical leader dictates. This applies to governments and other institutional structures as well as to individuals. Wrongs within rights must be tolerated in a morally sound democracy. In this way, toleration—at least of a morally constrained kind—is intrinsic to a sound democracy, but the virtue of tolerance requires more than meeting the minimal standards for preservation of free elections.

Tolerance and Wrongdoing

We cannot *determine* what counts as due tolerance apart from moral principles and associated rights. It is true that 'What should we tolerate?' can be used to mean roughly 'What should we include among liberty rights?' But even if these questions are taken to capture the same overt behavior, the question what our rights are is more basic than the question what we should tolerate. One way to see this is to note that violation of rights is a good ground, even if not always a conclusive ground, for *not* tolerating the wrongful behavior in question, whereas the point that something should not be tolerated is not in general a ground, and is never a basic ground, for denying a moral right to do it. Exercises of rights are at least minimally permissible; but as we have seen, some of these exercises are morally criticizable, deserve disapproval, and need not be unqualifiedly tolerated. Some should be (peaceably) opposed. Many other exercises of rights, however, do not *need* toleration; many should be applauded, not tolerated.

Where behavior should not be tolerated, there is perhaps even more variability in the appropriate response than in the case of obligatory toleration. Toleration requires resisting not only compulsion but also strong pressure and, more generally, interference with the tolerated behavior. But non-toleration can range from brutal slaughter of the innocent to unjustified criticism of political opponents; and *intolerance* as a stance can be a disposition to perform any of a wide range of deeds between lethal preventions and interfering remonstrances. A general point here is that where non-toleration is justified, the amount and kind of pressure used should be no greater than needed to prevent the wrongful behavior that—like most large-scale rights violations—is beyond toleration.

There are, however, certain rights violations, such as breaking promises to family members, that "we" outsiders, at least, should tolerate and perhaps even the victims should tolerate in certain special circumstances. From those we love we may properly tolerate violations of certain rights, especially when fulfilling them is a hardship for the others. And even where we should not tolerate them, outsiders who have the power to intervene may be unjustified in doing so. Some rights are not properly enforced at all. Some that are enforced should not be, partly because of *other* rights and partly because enforcement would be at best contrary to moral virtue—including tolerance. This applies to some religious conduct, such as certain calls to prayer, or ringing of bells, that citizens have a right to outlaw as annoyances. It also applies to the influence of religion in politics, as where we should recognize a right to act contrary to the principle of secular rationale; and (as illustrated already) in personal relationships examples abound.[4]

It would seem, then, that we need principles of conduct to determine a good set of laws; and we need a notion of rights, especially liberty rights, to determine what should be tolerated even if it is sometimes objectionable. A psychological account of tolerance, or any other account not guided by substantive ethical standards, cannot tell us what *should* be tolerated as opposed to what is tolerated. One way to see what should be tolerated and how is to articulate some important connections between toleration and forgiveness. Let us explore those.

III. Toleration and Forgiveness

If tolerance implies disapproval or at least a certain dislike; and if some of the conduct we tolerate we also regard as wrong, it becomes important to consider whether, in addition to requiring an appropriate attitude, morally well-grounded tolerance should lead to forgiving those wrongs one should tolerate.

It is also natural to connect the two notions because both concern how presumptive wrongdoing should be treated, and both belong to what might be called the irenic side of morality. They each embody both a negative attitude and abstention from coercion or certain other uses of force. Indeed, one might expect a forgiving person to be tolerant—though there is certainly no invariable connection here—and if a tolerant person is not by nature forgiving, forgivingness is at least a disposition that makes tolerance less stressful.

To focus the issue, I suggest that forgiveness of what one takes to be a wrong entails ceasing to hate or bear ill-will toward the perpetrator and, more positively, a disposition to relate to the perpetrator in a way appropriate to the person under the conditions preceding the wrong.[5] Consider a military case. Take a commander who tolerates sexual relationships among the troops but discovers that one soldier, a mature man, has drawn a young recruit of lower rank into a sexual relationship with him. Forgiveness does not require going to a neutral attitude, but does require forswearing anger and bitterness, and—if the offense has ceased—acquiring (in cases like this) a disposition to resume the professional conduct appropriate to the man's behavior before the relationship began.

This case illustrates that forgiveness does not entail approval of the conduct forgiven and that it does not require a readiness to resume completely normal relations with the person forgiven. The required change is specific to the case; it is not a change to a condition in which the forgiver should be approving or even neutral. Indeed, forgiveness, like tolerance, does not entail being guided by sound standards. A forgiving condition may itself call for forgiveness where the first instance of forgiveness is based on a mistaken belief that a wrong-doer has reformed. Forgiveness may also be naively bestowed on a person of constitutional malice, such as Shakespeare's Iago. As these cases show, we may need forgiveness for harboring an attitude that is misguided, even when, in forgiving a person who seems to us to have done wrong, we have achieved one good thing by overcoming the bitterness and resentment that went with the attitude.[6]

Forgiveness is akin to tolerance, but neither implies or automatically justifies the other. One might, for instance, forgive a deed once but then not tolerate its repetition. In some cases, however, as in strong friendships, forgiveness restores a level of respect and interaction that manifests mutual approval and may not be correctly described as one in which tolerance runs either way.

Forgiveness, unlike tolerance in some instances, is arguably not called for without repentance on the part of the offender. This is not to say that forgiveness would not be good even in many such cases; but there may be times when one is in no way morally criticizable for not forgiving a malicious and unrepentant offender—at least in sociopolitical as opposed to religious or highly personal contexts. In some personal contexts, forgiveness might be, as it were, *owed*. Tolerance certainly is owed for certain kinds of behavior—especially those to which there is a moral right—*rights-protected behavior*. This holds independently of whether those who owe tolerance feel that according it is potentially impermissible or even undesirable; and tolerance may also be owed where it extends to rights-protected wrongs for which the agent is in no way repentant.

IV. The Normative Standards for Democratic Toleration

So far, nothing has been said about the normative question of just what a democratic society should tolerate. Here we must bear in mind the distinction (made in Chapter 2) between what it has a right to do and what, all things considered, it ought to do. Rights entail a moral justification in the minimal sense that no one may properly prevent the acts to which there is a right. Call this *protective justification*. It contrasts with a justification that demands positive action—an *obligating justification*—as where one must restrain a friend about to do an ill-considered life-threatening deed. But we may have a right to do something, such as abstain from assisting an accident victim, and a corresponding (arguably equivalent) protective justification for doing it, even where we ought not to do this. This category of protectively justified acts we ought not to perform illustrates what I have called wrongs within rights.

These points apply to both moral and legal rights. This is not to say that, in the normative order, moral rights are not more basic than legal rights (though that is a plausible view). The two kinds are, however, quite different; and tolerance, like charity, may be a moral obligation even where it is not a legal one. It may also be desirable, even morally, where what is tolerated is, though not a violation of anyone's rights, also not rights-protected—such that the agent has a right to do the deed(s) in question. I will consider mainly moral issues, but some of these concern what laws we should have where the domain is one in which some citizens must tolerate others.

In considering the normative status of tolerance, it is essential to keep in mind that it is not a friendly attitude. Although it may be held toward friends regarding many things they do, tolerance is an attitude that, embodying disapproval or at least dislike, may strain relations between those who tolerate and those whose conduct they disapprove of. The question whether to tolerate, then, is not about just overt behavior; it also concerns what attitudes one should have.

Toleration and Rational Disagreement

The question of what to tolerate and how best to do so commonly arises when those facing it are considering people they do not regard as equally reasonable on the matters about which they differ. But suppose all the parties are fully rational.

Surely the ethics of citizenship in a pluralistic democracy must take account not only of actual disagreement between citizens who may or may not be equally rational, but also of the possibility of fully rational disagreement between *epistemic peers* relative to the matter in question. Roughly, epistemic peers are (rational) persons who are, in the matter in question, equally rational, possessed of the same relevant evidence, and equally conscientious in assessing that evidence. Rational disagreement between epistemic peers can occur not just inter-religiously—between people who differ in religion (or one or more of whom is not religious at all) but also intra-religiously.

If we think that a disagreement is with an epistemic peer and we wish to retain our position, we should try to find new evidence for it or at least to discover a basis for thinking the disputant is not as rational or as conscientious as we are in appraising the issue. But there may be times when the most reasonable conclusion is that there is epistemic parity between us and, for that reason, the disagreement cannot be readily resolved in one's favor. This may seem to many conscientious citizens to be how things stand on the permissibility of assisted suicide, capital punishment, or abortion.

What is the appropriate response to finding oneself in a situation of persisting disagreement with an apparent epistemic peer? One response is skepticism, concluding that neither party has knowledge or even justification. There could, however, be a difference in the disputants' conflicting justifications that neither can discover. But should we always suppose both that this is so and that our own view is rationally preferable to that of an apparent epistemic peer?

A quite different response to persisting disagreement in such cases is humility. Minimally, we might conclude that we might be mistaken or at least less justified than our peer is for holding a contrary position. Humility is a response that tends to prevent (though it need not always prevent) taking one's view as a basis for establishing coercive laws or public policies. In that way it gives some support to the idea that in sound democracies, liberty is the default position: the preferred position when there is not a cogent reason for coercion. With all this in mind, I propose a

> *Principle of rational disagreement*: The justification of coercion in a given instance is (other things equal) inversely proportional to the strength of the evidence for epistemic parity among disputants who disagree on whether coercion in that instance is warranted.

The idea applies to governmental as well as individual acts. Imagine two political parties disputing legislation. There may be epistemic peers on both sides. Suppose, to simplify matters, just two individuals are in question: X has power over Y and is considering forcing Y to A. Roughly, the principle implies that X's justification for coercing Y to A for reason(s) R is weaker in proportion to the strength of the evidence for the parity of X and Y regarding their disagreement on whether R constitutes adequate reason to require Y to A.

It should be clear that this principle is supported, as are other elements in my view, by considerations of reciprocity. The principle of rational disagreement is certainly in the spirit of "Do unto others." Suppose we are averse to doing something that we are urged by our employer to do. It is personally objectionable to us, but we are given a plausible argument for it, though not one so convincing that it eliminates our hesitation. In cases like this we can acquiesce in having to do it if the argument comes from someone we consider on a par with us in the matter; we often realize we would expect the same response to us. We would resent being pressured or forced to do it given the same argument from someone we consider unreasonable or significantly less informed than we are in the matter.[7] But where a requirement comes from someone we consider an epistemic peer in the matter, tolerance of what we dislike comes more easily and may have little effect on our conduct or relationships.

Rational Disagreement and Coercion

The principle of rational disagreement is a useful adjunct to the principle of secular rationale—the principle of natural reason—but is not essential to the appropriate employment of the latter. The rational disagreement principle may require some sophistication but not, I think, more than is possessed by a competent high school graduate in many educationally "advanced" countries. The principle also helps to nourish a kind of humility and respect for others' views that is a desirable element in democratic societies of any kind.

The principle of rational disagreement does not specify *how* weak the justification for coercion becomes as the case for parity becomes stronger. If the case is conclusive—though that would be at best rare—I suggest that the obligation to tolerate becomes overriding. This is in good part because the justification for coercion in a given instance approaches zero as the strength of the case for epistemic parity among disputants who disagree on whether the relevant coercion in that instance is warranted approaches conclusiveness. This point seems to hold in interpersonal relations generally. But I also take it to apply in governmental matters arising in democratic societies. The principle thus clarifies the sense in which liberty is the default position in a sound democracy.

In the light of these points, we can formulate a more specific principle applicable to both individual conduct and governmental action, such as legislation and public policy determination:

> *The principle of toleration*: If it not reasonable for proponents of coercion in a given matter to consider themselves epistemically superior in that matter to supporters of the

> corresponding liberty, then in that matter the former have
> a prima facie obligation to tolerate rather than coerce.[8]

In practice, the value of this principle in the life of a democracy depends on the conscientiousness of those with the power and inclination to coerce. If unconscientious, they would readily think it reasonable to take defenders of the liberty in question to be less than epistemic peers in the relevant matter. If conscientious, they would tend to resist this view if there is any serious question at all about who is right.

Indeed, highly conscientious government officials—or virtually any conscientious, rational, and tolerant person with coercive power over others, as in the case of government officials—will, if unopposed by actual disputants, try to think of the best *hypothetical* defense they can construct in favor of the liberty they would restrict or eliminate. They would then extend the principle to that case. A conscientious search for the kind of justification needed for coercion does not necessarily conclude when the best counterarguments actually given are overriding. We should not coerce—and are generally averse to being coerced—even when there is a discernible prospect of finding overriding counterarguments. Good ethics requires exploring not just the evidence presented but relevant hypothetical cases.

Tolerance in Religious Matters

Given that toleration of religious practices that some find disagreeable or even immoral is a kind that a morally sound democracy must maintain, it is appropriate to ask whether some of the religions it tolerates are committed to *intolerance* of outsiders and whether that is a ground for at least selective intolerance of those religions. Someone might think that if, as has been argued regarding Christianity and other religions, a religion is committed to taking those who reject it to be consigned to eternally disastrous consequences, it thereby licenses whatever kinds of compulsion are necessary to achieve doctrinal and behavioral conformity with its saving provisions. But licensing such compulsion is not a commitment of Christian-theology, even though, historically, some church leaders have so interpreted their religion. Christians and many other theists, for instance, may take human freedom to be given by God for the purpose of allowing people to determine their ultimate fate for themselves. This is not the place to explore whether, on the most plausible reading of, say, the Christian Bible (chiefly the New Testament), its overall thrust does not imply the damnation of those who reject Christianity. There are, however, two points to be made here that bear on how toleration may be viewed from the perspective of Christianity and presumably other monotheistic religions.

The first point is that natural theology should be given significant authority in determining what one is committed to by virtue of an intelligent adherence to an Abrahamic religion—Judaism, Christianity, and Islam. Indeed, as I have argued in Chapter 1, even given just the assumption (generally made in works of natural theology) of God's being all-knowing, all-powerful, and perfectly good, it is reasonable to expect that in a world under divine sovereignty, we would be created with a capacity to determine by natural reason basic principles for civilized life in human society.

Second, there in fact is a set of broad moral principles that are rationally acceptable, consonant with attributing moral authority to God, and indeed supported by much literature in major religious traditions. I take these to include the kinds of commonsense principles articulated by W. D. Ross: principles of justice and non-injury, veracity and fidelity, beneficence and self-improvement, and reparation and gratitude.[9] (These include at least most of the directives contained in the ethical injunctions of the Ten Commandments.) One apparent implication of these principles is that, as perfectly good, God would not unjustly punish people, whether for "unbelief" or for any other wrong. It might also be argued that torture, including the kind sometimes portrayed as entailed by damnation, is *never* punitively just; but even apart from that plausible view, *infinitely* extended torture is surely disproportionate to any wrongdoing of the kind supposed to merit it according to common readings of certain Biblical passages.

It seems to me, then, that Christians are not committed to practicing, or even approving of, intolerance of atheism or of all conflicting religions, and I cannot see that the same should not hold for certain other theistic religions. My main point here, however, is that a sound democracy should tolerate both religion and opposition to it—with the understanding that toleration is always to be governed by moral principles calling not only for liberty but for protection from harm to persons in its exercise. This stance would allow for legal protection of intolerant *attitudes* on the part of both the religious and the anti-religious but would require behavioral tolerance of both those attitudes and any conduct they generate that is within the limits of liberty.

If we take liberty to be a moral and legal right, it will be evident that the level of freedom to which a morally sound democracy is committed will protect the conduct of some in a way that will deeply annoy, even aggrieve, others. It seems intrinsic to a sound democracy that some such conduct must be tolerated. Mill mentioned fornication and gambling.[10] Recall the part of his harm principle that reads: " . . . the sole end for which mankind are warranted, individually or collectively, in interfering with the liberty of action of any of their number, is self-protection . . . to prevent harm to others." Parentalistic interferences are ruled out except where those who may harm themselves are children or (presumably) irrational. Mill apparently saw no harms to others (i.e., non-participants) that would justify preventing fornication and gambling. Suppose we add not only controversial medical practices like stem cell research and assisted suicide but also religious practices ranging from broadcasting calls to prayer over loud speakers (as mosques characteristically do) to modes of dress that announce religious affiliation and, in some eyes, symbolize the oppression of women. How far should toleration go in such matters?[11]

Let me pursue some of the aspects of tolerance of concern in this chapter in relation to one important area: the workplace.

V. Religion in the Workplace as a Test Case for a Theory of Toleration

In discussing toleration in connection with religious practices in a democratic society I want to go beyond Mill's harm principle. That principle establishes at most what freedom rights we have as citizens, but the question of toleration goes further. We have already seen that toleration implies dislike or an attitude of disapproval, and such attitudes themselves are morally appraisable. We may oppose the admirable and tolerate the intolerable. Should we merely tolerate certain liberties, as Mill apparently thought regarding fornication and gambling, which he saw as protected by his harm principle? Moreover, there are domains of conduct in which we have more freedom to restrict behavior than government does. Not only families but also private businesses and privately held organizations like foundations are cases in point.

I will presuppose here that (as I argued in Chapters 1–3) in church-state relations governments should protect religious liberty, treat different religious groups equally, and remain neutral toward religion, neither preferring the religious over the secular nor vice-versa. These principles should suggest a variety of applications to governmental employers and their employees; and if we consider public schools an educational workplace, we have already seen applications of them there, in relation to teaching evolutionary biology. This section mainly concerns "private" business, but governmental employment is also briefly considered.

Any well-ordered business has this much in common with a government: it is rule-governed, even if only loosely, and, depending on (among other things) how readily employees can find alternative jobs, it may have coercive power over them. A major concern of ethics is what constitutes a fair system of rules; another of its major concerns is how coercive power may be limited. On both counts, employment practices in business raise some of the same ethical problems as government employment.

To be sure, there is significant disanalogy between employer-employee relations in private versus governmental cases. (1) In the former cases employees are not as such part of a voting constituency, though they are major stakeholders in their employing organization and there may be a sense in which they are one group in a broadly conceived constituency to which their employers are responsible.[12] Employees can be part of a voting constituency if they are *stockholders*; but even these voting rights are not comparable to those of citizens, for instance because of a narrower range of coercive powers in those chosen as managers. (2) The contractual relations a business has with employees commonly do not prohibit "establishment" and, for some private companies, may provide for a good measure of it. Indeed, since churches are major employers, clearly there are some private employers for whom a strong preference on a religious basis *is* permissible.

In the case of private employers, the analogy to government is matched—and in some ways counterbalanced—by the analogy to an individual citizen. Indeed, businesses are sometimes owned by a single individual. Even when they are not individually owned, the liberty guaranteed to free associations extends to them. Let us first consider private businesses without publicly traded shares, especially those that are "closely held." (This is a vague notion, but its vagueness should not affect any significant point in our discussion.) One plausible ethical standard here—a *standard of managerial discretion*—is *the private business standard*: Privately held business may give some degree of preference to religious persons or groups as such. Let me explain.

The degree of preference may be high, but ethics does not allow unlimited preference for a religious group, irrespective of competence, character, and other variables important for the success of the business and the well-being of society. Even establishment of a religion, moreover, does not justify discrimination on any other basis, a point widely acknowledged in some countries that still have an established church, such as England. Nondiscrimination—or at least a kind of it—is a moral obligation of businesses. Even if their owners or managers do give some preference to a particular religion, they should not in any other respect disadvantage employees who pursue—within morally acceptable limits—another religion. This implies tolerance in attitude as well as in behavior. Managerial attitudes are a major factor in making a place of work comfortable for religious and other nonconformists.

With businesses, we again find differences from free democratic government as committed to the liberty, equality, and neutrality principles. For whereas a democracy may not prefer one religion over another and may not even prefer the religious as such over the non-religious, privately held companies may. They may—within limits and given openness regarding the operation of the policy—prefer even a particular denomination in hiring and promotion. These limits are difficult to describe. It is one thing to prefer, say, a candidate for employment with the religion of the owners if other things are equal in terms of qualifications for the job; it is another to do so when someone religiously different is far better qualified for the job in question.

An *employer* need not be what is normally termed a *business*, but government employers such as the U.S. Postal System are plainly in competition with businesses, and, whether they are viewed as businesses or not, they must operate under management policies that take account of religion. The policies appropriate from an ethical point of view vary widely, but here it is reasonable to formulate a *principle of managerial restraint* bearing on church-state relations:

> *The governmental employer principle.* Governmental employers should adopt management policies that accord with the liberty, equality, and neutrality principles.

Here it is the neutrality principle that is most likely to be questioned or suspended in special cases and is most likely to be difficult to clarify by appeal to even the many pertinent laws that a country like the United States may have. May a post office in a small, predominantly Christian town put up Christmas decorations? Despite appearances, the neutrality principle may allow this and similar kinds of religious expression under certain conditions. If there are also holiday decorations of a secular character and the Christmas decorations do not include religious content presented as endorsed, the *setting* may be neutral toward religion as opposed to secularity, and religion need not be favored over secularity.

The practice may still fail to meet the *equality* standard, however, if no religion other than Christianity is represented side by side with the secular symbols (or on the relevant celebratory occasions). Treating one religion on a par with the secular, even if it is consistent with a plausible understanding of the neutrality principle may still have effects that favor this religion over others. Suppose, however, that although no other religion is represented, this is only because no other has practitioners among the citizenry of the community in question. Should the minority of secular citizens (or any citizens who disapprove of the governmental omission) be intolerant, say enlisting legal help in banning the decorations? This would be within their legal and perhaps moral rights, but it might be ethically undesirable. The situation could be one in which the imbalance is unintentional and protest would be counterproductive.

In the light of this kind of departure from equality and perhaps neutrality as well, it seems reasonable for government—as it may be for certain businesses—either to sponsor no official representation of religious symbols or to give all the religious traditions present in the community some representation, and in such a way that their prominence resembles the proportions of the relevant population in the community belonging to those traditions. One might here speak of a *principle of proportionate inclusion* as governing displays of religious symbols in a governmental workplace—and arguably applicable to certain large publicly held companies as well. The principle calls for including religious symbols roughly in proportion to the number of people they represent in the relevant community (mainly employees in some cases, especially in non-public company space, but in other cases including customers and sometimes suppliers).

We have so far not considered very large, publicly traded companies, such as GE, IBM, and Merck. In some countries, such companies are legal persons; but because of their size, the diversity of their workforce, and the impersonal relation of most of their stockholders to management, the appropriate ethical standards for their treatment of religion are less permissive than those for closely held companies. As a first approximation, we might adopt this quasi-governmental principle:

> *The default principle for publicly held companies:* Publicly held companies should abide by policies toward religion that conform to corporate counterparts of the liberty, equality, and neutrality principles.

The reason why this is the default principle is that there may be adequate reason for departures from it and for policies more like those of certain privately held businesses. Even a large publicly traded company is owned by its stockholders, who, by virtue of ownership, have special rights and may in special cases ask for a certain policy. If, for instance, enough stockholders of the Target Stores wanted to reinstate the policy of allowing the Salvation Army (which is religiously affiliated) to ring bells and solicit contributions, this would provide good reason for management to allow it.

Like any company, a large publicly held one also has special responsibilities toward its employees. In matters of policy toward religion, as in certain other important matters, it is appropriate for management to consult stockholders as well as employees. This may be done in various ways (and deserves separate treatment not possible here). Given the technological resources of many companies, electronic communication is likely to open up new opportunities for ascertaining needs and preferences. In any case, it is reasonable for directors who are elected by stockholders to indicate their managerial position on religion in the workplace. This may often center on affirming a nondiscrimination policy as regards religious applicants and employees, but neutrality may be included by adding the non-religious to the description of the groups with respect to which there is to be no discrimination.

Quite apart from such formal procedures, management at any level can exercise judgment as to what is appropriate for the company in relation to religion. Such judgment should take account of a number of important variables. One is the composition and apparent preferences of the employees. Another is the preferences, so far as they can be determined, of stockholders. Still another variable—not entirely independent of the former two—is degree of fit with the mission statement and ethics code of the company.

If there is a broad conclusion warranted here regarding tolerance of religion in the workplace, it is that—with the exceptions noted for privately owned businesses—behavioral tolerance should be as extensive as is compatible with non-governmental counterparts of the liberty, equality, and neutrality principles, and attitudinal tolerance should be kept consistent with mutual respect and peaceful coexistence. A morally sound democracy must protect liberties whose exercise is repugnant to some. The expression of those liberties should be tolerated in a civilized way even where disapproval is expressed and dissuasion is attempted. In the workplace, however, the focus of activity should be the common concern with getting the job done, and this can make it easier to keep conflicting attitudes toward religion generally in the background.

VI. Cosmopolitanism as a Framework for Tolerance

I have been speaking so far of tolerance within a nation-state, but my case for toleration is based on ethics and political philosophy. From that wide point of view, should we restrict our consideration of tolerance to nations and their citizens? Indeed, if private businesses must observe moral standards not enforced by law, might nation-states and multinational, publicly owned companies be obligated to do likewise? Here, of course, there may be no international law with the binding force over nations that the laws of a nation have over its citizens. But there are international ethical standards, and I take the United Nations Declaration of Human Rights to express some of them. Freedom of religion figures prominently among these rights.[13]

Cosmopolitanism versus Nationalism

The strength of any international body with legal authority over nation-states is not just a matter of the proportion of those states that are generally cooperating members; it is also affected by the level of cosmopolitanism exhibited by those members, especially the more powerful ones. How should we conceive cosmopolitanism, and does ethics require endorsing some measure of it? The main variable that, in my view, determines the strength of a cosmopolitan versus nationalistic position is the relative importance it ascribes to human as opposed to national concerns. Nationalists tend to give priority to specifically *national* concerns, and extreme nationalists tend to adhere to the view epitomized in "my country right or wrong." Cosmopolitans tend to give priority to specifically *human* concerns: such things as the elements of physical and psychological well-being on the part of persons everywhere. These concerns properly motivate policy decisions independently of the welfare of any particular nation. Human concerns would be important for people even in a "state of nature." Those concerns have high priority in the ethics of the world's major religious, but (given the autonomy of ethics defended in Chapter 1) the human concerns central for understanding the contrast between nationalism and cosmopolitanism do not normatively depend on values that are intrinsically religious.

It is both natural and plausible to assume that the value of nations and other social structures is *derivative*. Nations and other institutional structures derive their value from their role in serving people—roughly, in promoting the common good. This is certainly how cosmopolitans tend to see the matter. On the plausible versions of cosmopolitanism, it is people who have *basic* moral status; nations have derivative moral status, much as their agency itself is derivative from that of individuals who occupy the roles in which they determine national policy, sign treaties, and declare states of emergency. In Kant's language, persons are ends in themselves. This implies that they can never be properly treated merely as means to the glory of nations. The common good is that of people, not that of nations in the abstract.

On a still wider view likely to be held by cosmopolitans, and also independently plausible, all non-personal values are subordinate to personal ones. Nations, for instance, properly exist for the benefit of persons—"for the people," as the famous sketch of democracy has it—not the other way around. This too seems to treat individuals as more basically valuable than any abstract structures such as nations. Broadly speaking, then, cosmopolitanism gives some degree of priority to the interests of humanity over those of nations, and indeed of people over governments. The stronger the priority, the stronger the cosmopolitanism.[14]

Suppose there is no perfectly general answer to the question whether ethics allows giving some degree of preference, even if very weak preference, to one's own nation in cases of conflicting interests. We may still say that *by and large* extreme nationalism tends to pay too little attention to obligations of beneficence toward other peoples—a kind of obligation most major ethical views acknowledge, at least where this collective obligation is taken to be a consequence of an obligation of beneficence to the individuals constituting a "people." But what we might call moderate nationalism need not do this. In one form, it simply prefers the interests of the nation in question when other things are approximately equal. Moderate cosmopolitanism, however, tends *not* to do this. It is, as it were, pledged to seek the well-being of all peoples and to accord that goal some priority over the well-being of those in any one nation.

A high degree of effort in this transnational, cosmopolitan quest is endorsed by at least the major ethical views and probably by all of the major religions as well, including Christianity, Judaism, and Islam. The rise of the modern nation-state has spurred extreme nationalism in many quarters; globalization invites—and perhaps is forcing many—to reconsider their historical commitment to this outlook. Most nations still need some measure of patriotism for optimal flourishing, but the only kind of patriotism that is morally justifiable is one leavened by concern for all peoples.[15]

Religious Tolerance in International Affairs

Are the principles of liberty, equality, and neutrality a good guide for international toleration in matters of religion, whether by nation-states or by international bodies with authority over them? If we take them to express strong prima facie standards, rather than absolute ones generating indefeasible obligations, they are. But I have already noted that human sacrifice and racial discrimination are not protected by the liberty principle. These practices, then, should not be tolerated. To say that, however, leaves open just what kinds of preventive action is warranted by such practices. What justifies coercion within a society—which may simply outlaw the practices—may not do so internationally. There may be no sufficiently strong international legal framework, and nontoleration may have to come in the form of economic and other pressures.

If, however, we had an international governmental institution with sufficient commitment from member communities, the legal possibilities might be similar to what they are in nation-states. I do not mean to endorse a strong cosmopolitanism on which there is a world government with universal powers parallel to those of nations over their own citizens. I leave open whether this is a good idea for the future. No such overall governance of the world is required for an international body to have the authority and power to enforce certain minimal standards of decency. That much cosmopolitanism seems a worthy goal, but achieving it will require individual nations to give up a measure of their sovereignty. For instance, they might have to supply military and economic assistance to an international effort to prevent the kinds of human rights violations that we have seen in, for instance, the Darfur region of Sudan.

Without an international body of the kind I am projecting, individual nations may have to tolerate much that they disapprove of at the level of abstaining from force; but this does not imply toleration at the level of voluntary association or attitudinal expression. Toleration at the international level does not, for instance, imply a willingness to trade with the tolerated nation or organization or to abstain from peaceful criticism of them. Even powerful sanctions are possible without military intervention. Here the cooperation of many nations may be required to achieve significant results. In my view, non-cooperation in imposing justified sanctions is a form of tacit toleration that is inappropriate to international treatment of nations in which human rights violations are not adequately fought.

Internationally as well as nationally, then, tolerance in both attitude and behavior is a necessity of contemporary life. We cannot live in peace in a world of such wide disagreement and cultural disparity without tolerating much that we disapprove of. But even where behavioral tolerance is obligatory, attitudinal tolerance may be unjustified: some conduct, especially in private or religiously protected settings, that should not be prevented should also be disapproved of and even subject to public criticism. A sufficiently developed ethical theory should set minimal limits on liberty but should also posit obligations to exercise liberty not merely within our rights but with respect for others. We should take no comfort in being merely tolerated by those we respect and should not tax them beyond reason; but we should also distinguish between the moral disapproval that warrants tolerance where coercive prevention is ruled out and the prejudices that yield toleration only because we are unwilling to use force to impose our preferences on those we otherwise favor, as where, for the sake of alliances, people who hold political power ignore oppression of women and other rights violations. The theory of tolerance should guide us not just in determining the limits of conduct, but also in formulating the ideals by which we may improve it.

VII. Civic Virtue and Democratic Participation

The previous chapters have affirmed the autonomy of ethics from religion and of religion from ethics even if not from conceptions of the good. But the high degree of mutual autonomy of ethics and religion does not imply their irrelevance to each other, and I have argued for the possibility of integration between moral and religious commitments in individuals and for the possibility of liberal accommodation of religion without the cost of utter neutrality toward the good. But more remains to be said about how, in the thinking and political conduct of individual citizens, ethics and religion can be integrated. I am especially interested in how such integration is possible for *religious* citizens in a pluralistic democracy, and I will begin with a focus on how certain such citizens might conceive and practice civic virtue—the kind of virtue of character appropriate to citizenship and to the public conduct that should go with it.

Civic Virtue

I presuppose here that a virtue is a certain kind of character trait, one appropriate to pursuing the particular good with respect to which the virtue counts as such. The virtue of tolerance, for instance, might have, as the central good that guides it, the value of self-realization: of living one's life in a freely chosen, constructive way. Thus, some understanding of autonomy is essential for determining what counts as tolerance, just as some understanding of the well-being of others is essential for determining what counts as beneficence. Similarly, understanding of certain kind of equal treatment is essential for determining what constitutes justice in a person with power over others.[16]

A virtue may be more or less deeply rooted in a person. It may also be grounded in religious as well as secular elements of character, or in both. Beneficence, for instance, might arise in a person through internalization of utilitarian, Kantian, or

Biblical standards, or—as is more likely in the upbringing of children in modern democracies—through internalizing a combination of elements from these or other normative stances. Similarly, utilitarianism, or Kant's Categorical Imperative, or the Biblical love commandments, or some combination of these standards may be cited to *justify* the view that beneficence is indeed a virtue in character or an obligation in action. Certain justificatory elements from these and other perspectives, then, can be combined.

Furthermore, the *motivation* that goes with a virtue may have more than one ground. Beneficence may be rooted in both religious devotion and commitment to moral principles. Moreover, it is quite possible for motivation to act on a virtue to rest mainly on one source, such as a set of religious commitments, while the agent's conception of what justifies such acts rests mainly on another source. Motivation and justification should ideally have much the same roots. But the roots of one may, without incongruity, be quite different from the roots of the other. Still, new growth and regrowth, either on the normative side of justificatory grounds, or on the motivational side of causal grounds, can be stimulated by education and dialogue, and both kinds of growth are nearly always possible.

In any virtue, both cognitive and motivational elements are central. A virtuous person, say one with veracity, must have certain beliefs. Some would say, indeed, that these beliefs must constitute *knowledge*, for instance knowledge a candid person has of when it is appropriate to express a religious conviction in a non-denominational political discussion. But I take such discriminativeness to be more a matter of knowing *how*—of behavioral knowledge—than of knowing *that*, propositional knowledge. Virtuous people must also have desires appropriate to the virtue, such as, in the case of fidelity, a desire to stand by friends.[17] Both beliefs and certain related desires are essential to the kind of wide-ranging and deep commitments that make a person religious or moral or both. One of my aims is to show how citizens can integrate both kinds of commitments and, on that basis, achieve civic virtue.

What, then, is civic virtue? It is the trait that underlies good citizenship when the conduct in question is grounded in the *character* of the citizen and not, for instance, a manifestation of merely self-interested cooperation. The cultivation of civic virtue is to be expected in anyone committed to the intuitively sound moral standards I have stressed. Consider the common-sense moral principles discussed earlier, positing obligations of justice and non-injury, veracity and fidelity, beneficence and self-improvement, and reparation and gratitude. A commitment to the principle of justice, for instance, tends to prevent free-riding, which is a paradigm of unfairness. A commitment to the principle of fidelity tends to prevent violating one's agreements and, more subtly, heightens one's sense of obligations beyond those undertaken by explicit promise. A commitment to the principle of beneficence enhances the tendency to cooperate with and support others. Justice, fidelity, and beneficence, taken together, go a good way toward sustaining civic virtue, but this is not the place to argue the point in detail even for them, much less for the overall set of intuitive obligations. In part, this is because my special concern is how civic virtue should be developed by religious citizens in a democracy. Many major religions require what, from their perspective, constitutes good citizenship. To give us a definite example of wide interest, I focus on Christianity, conceived broadly enough to be seen as similar to other religions.

The Love Commandments as Standards for Civic Virtue

Imagine a Christian citizen who takes as central in public life Jesus's commandments—also important in the Hebrew Bible (the Old Testament)—to love God with all our heart, all our soul, and all our mind, and to love our neighbors as ourselves (Matthew 22:37–39; cf. Mark 12:29–31; Leviticus 19:18; and

Deuteronomy 6:4). Any Christian, Jew, or other religious person for whom the Bible is theologically central will have more specific standards that guide the effort to obey these commands. Still, at least for Christians, the love commandments should have a kind of priority in sociopolitical matters. The word 'love' is easily misunderstood here as implying strong affection; what is intended (toward others) is apparently something like *agape* love, the fraternal kind that goes with empathy and beneficence.

A difficulty with these commandments is to determine just what they require us to *do*?[18] On the one hand, although there are many kinds of acts of love, love is not an act at all; on the other hand, it is not clear what is meant by commands whose objects are *not* acts. I can raise my hands at will, and so can do it on command. But consider commanding people to love a person they hate. How are we even to understand this? Does a command to love make clear sense even as applied to an acquaintance one finds perfectly pleasant, yet does not love? Properly understood, it does make sense.

The commandment to love may seem not to make clear sense because we cannot love at will. One important point is that even if we lack direct positive control over emotions, and hence cannot bring them into being at will, we *sometimes* have direct negative control over them. I cannot fear at will, but I sometimes can simply *overcome* fear by an act of will—by "resolving" not to be afraid, to put it more naturally. Similarly, if we cannot love at will, perhaps we can sometimes expel hatred at will. That can often enable what is good in us to prevail in a way that allows love to come into being.

Even apart from the possibility of doing at will things that make way for love to grow, there *are* of course *acts* of love. Acts of love, like the acts of charity called for by civic virtue, may be commanded. But those that deserve the name, those that merit being called acts of love by their *constitution* rather than their appearance, are not always achievable at will, if they ever are. The constitution of these acts that bespeak love includes their motivational grounding; their appearance is a matter of what act-type they belong to. It is similar with civic virtue: to count as manifesting civic virtue, making a sacrifice for one's community must be done for an other-regarding reason, and it requires forgoing something one wants. It is not a matter of mere behavior, such as handing over a sum of money.

It will help to distinguish between *acting on a command*— say, to love one's neighbor—and *fulfilling* a command. In the case of the command to love one's neighbor, fulfillment requires both actually loving another person—in some sense— and acting in a way appropriate to this love. The end state is not entirely external (a matter of overt behavior), and the route to it is also important. We are to create relationships, and in them we are to do the right kinds of deeds *for* the right kinds of reasons. We do have positive and sometimes direct voluntary control of at least many of the relevant preparatory acts; but we do not have direct voluntary control of our motivation. The mere performance of the kinds of deeds appropriate to love is at best enough to achieve the appearance of doing what is Biblically commanded. In different terms, the love commandments impose obligations of *manner*, not just obligations of *matter*.[19]

Religious and Secular Understandings of Civic Virtue

Since civic virtue is my central concern here, I want to consider some approaches to its exercise in the political life of individuals and, more broadly, in international relations. I take it that a person of faith who is also a conscientious citizen will, on the basis of religious ideals, want to have a positive influence on society and to play a constructive role in making this world better. Christians, Jews, and Muslims can, to be sure, be guided by certain secular ethical standards, such as those proposed in this book. Suppose, then, that I have a moral theory which I take to be compatible with my Christian commitments (or other religious commitments), but I also want to be guided in my sociopolitical life by the love commandments. Are there any constraints I must recognize?

There are two importantly different kinds of case here, coercive and non-coercive conduct. Giving to a charity that peacefully provides medical services to those who cannot otherwise get them is not coercive. Voting to outlaw assisted suicide is coercive. To move from the domestic to the international realm, promoting foreign aid to fight malnutrition rather than fund highway construction is not coercive, or is minimally so. Advocating military action against a foreign country does support coercion and may be conceived as itself indirectly coercive. Our concern here is not religiously grounded *non-coercive* action. It is acts that restrict liberty that are our problem. Many people are prone to violence in the service of their holy causes. How can citizens, especially religious citizens, at once fulfill their highest ideals and balance religious and secular considerations?

Consider religious citizens who, among other things, seek to fulfill the love commandments in an atmosphere of liberty and religious pluralism. They need not ignore their religious understanding of their obligations. Moreover, in the light of the existence of moral as well as religiously based obligations to fulfill interpersonal religious commitments, and indeed in the light of what might be considered religious virtue, I have already proposed, as a companion to the principle of secular rationale, the principle of religious rationale, which applies particularly to citizens whose religions have (as do Christianity, Judaism, and Islam) an ethic that extends to large segments of sociopolitical conduct. It articulates a prima facie obligation not to advocate or support any law or public policy that restricts human conduct, unless the religious citizen has, and is willing to offer, adequate *religiously* acceptable reason for this advocacy or support.

The two rationale principles each provide for adherence to the other. Each requires having reasons grounded in its own point of view; but neither excludes the importance of the other viewpoint. Thus, the principle of secular rationale does not preclude having, or being motivated by, religious reasons for the same actions or thinking the former more important than secular reasons. The requirement is *inclusive* relative to secular reason; it is not *exclusive* of religious reasons. Counterparts of these points apply to the principle of religious rationale. It does not exclude secular reasons. It simply requires including adequate religious ones.

The two rationale principles express a substantive ideal to be internalized in civic virtue. But they differ in that whereas the primary audience for secular reasons is citizens regardless of religious conviction, the primary audience for religious reasons is citizens who are religious—especially those who need to see their sociopolitical conduct as religiously justified—or citizens of any worldview who are specially concerned with the role of religious considerations in justifying that conduct. This difference in addressees does not, however, undermine a further similarity between the principles. Just as a secular reason need not be secular in its *content,* as opposed to its evidential *grounds,* an adequate religiously acceptable reason need not be religious in its content, though it may be religious in both its content and its grounds. A secular reason might, for example, be to the effect that *religious* liberty requires allowing vouchers for tuition reimbursement to be given by the government to students who choose Christian schools over government ones. This consideration and other secular reasons might move religious citizens as well as some non-religious citizens.

Even a religious person moved by an explicitly religious reason, say that God forbids killing other people, need not be thinking of a particular religion. Consider the moral imperatives among the Ten Commandments. These might be invoked by people of quite different overall religious views. These commandments can provide religiously acceptable reasons for many believers, but the directives themselves, as opposed to the text in which they are presented, do not mention God. The directives are *religiously endorsed,* but *conceptually secular.*[20]

Civic Virtue and Rationalization

Both rationale principles articulate standards of civic virtue; but each can be followed in a *way* that does not *express* civic virtue. For neither principle rules out having reasons that figure in one's conduct only as *rationalizations.* Suppose someone offers exploitation of the poor as a reason for outlawing assisted suicide. If the person is *motivated* in opposing it only by a conviction that it is against God's will, then offering the reason is only a civic rationalization and does not express civic virtue. Such a rationalization may even be combined with self-deception. Granted, self-deceptive rationalizers may *believe* themselves to be motivated by the cited reason and need not, in the ordinary sense, lie. But the principle of secular rationale does not even preclude knowingly offering reasons that one realizes do not motivate one.

It is even possible to take a reason to be good, to hold the view for which one offers it as support, and still be motivated to hold or act on the view *by* some *other* reason. This is probably not uncommon where one is citing reasons drawn from someone *else's* point of view in an effort to get them to join one in a position or action supported by their reasons but not embraced by them. We can attribute evidential adequacy to considerations without taking them into our perspective as motivators along with our own reasons. It is natural to call this kind of persuasive attempt *leveraging by reasons.* It can but need not be manipulative; and, properly used, it is a good adjunct to the kind of civilized attempts to change belief or behavior that go with democratic discussion.[21]

At this point you might ask: Why should motivation matter ethically if the quality of our justifying reasons for our conduct is adequate? From the perspective of virtue ethics, at least, it does matter. Insofar as we are thinking of the advocacy in question or other public behavior as supposed to be action *from virtue*, we should look not just at what *kind* of act it is and what can be said for it abstractly, but also at how it is *grounded* in the agent's *character*.[22] Aristotle distinguished—as any virtue theorist should—actions that *express* virtue from those not virtuously performed but merely of the right type. And Kant, a paradigmatic rule theorist very different from Aristotle, similarly distinguished acting merely in *conformity* with duty and acting *from* duty. For reasons overlapping theirs, we should differentiate actions from civic virtue and actions merely in conformity with it.

Civic Virtue and Reasons for Action

The principles of secular rationale and religious rationale focus on reasons we have and give for actions or beliefs, but reasons we are actually moved by, whether we offer them or not, are, as illustrated at several points so far, also ethically important. We like to know what motivates others in important matters on which we must determine laws or policy. We should and often do want to know what our own motives are in such matters. Conscientious citizens should consider not just what they want to do in political matters and what reasons they have to do it, but *why* they want to do it. This kind of reflection contributes to making good decisions, facilitates communication, and helps to create an impression of self-knowledge and sincerity in political discussion and debate.

With all this in mind we may see the ethics of citizenship as adding a motivational condition to the secular rationale principle, namely:

> *The principle of secular motivation*: Citizens in a democracy have a (prima facie) obligation to abstain from advocacy or support of a law or public policy that restricts human conduct, unless in advocating or supporting it they are sufficiently *motivated* by adequate secular reason.[23]

Sufficiency of motivation here implies that some set of secular reasons is motivationally sufficient for the action. Thus, such reasons explain *why* the agent acts (even if there is also another explaining factor). Second, the motivational strength of some set of secular reasons is such that the agent would do the thing in question even if, all else remaining equal, the agent's other reasons were eliminated.

This principle is important, though less so than the secular rationale principle, to the partial ethics of citizenship that I am proposing. Acting in accord with the rationale principle tends to assure that the right kind of thing is done; acting on the motivation called for by the motivation principle need not improve the chance of this but only assures that the citizen has the kind of motivation that bespeaks civic virtue. Important though that is as an aim of conduct, it is even more important that we treat one another in the right ways, whatever our motivation.

The motivation principle is also more difficult to interpret and apply than the rationale principle. Let us explore it in a concrete case. To begin with, since an argument can be tacitly religious, say evidentially or motivationally, without being religious in content, one might fail to adhere to at least the secular motivation principle even in offering arguments that on their face are neither religious nor fail to provide an adequate secular reason for their conclusion. Think of the genetic argument for the personhood of the zygote: roughly, that since all the genetic information for its development into a person is present at conception, the zygote *is* a person at that point. Suppose that some people who offer this argument are not sufficiently motivated by the secular considerations cited in it, those just mentioned, and (quite apart from whether the argument is objectively sound) would not find the argument convincing apart from their underlying religious beliefs. They might, for example, conceive the zygote as ensouled by God at the moment of its formation or might simply be brought up thinking of all human life as sacred—in a sense implying creation by God.

There are two cases here. In one, I realize that the secular reason does not motivate me. I might perceive that, for instance, the idea of ensoulment is what really convinces me on the abortion question. Here the secular reason is presented—sincerely, to be sure—as a rationalization for the position held on a religious basis. In the other case, I do not realize that the secular reason is not motivating for me. There the presentation of the reason is an unconscious rationalization. A rationalization can be good, in that the ground it invokes may actually justify what it is intended to support. But it is quite characteristic of rationalizations to be unsuccessful attempts to justify. This is common in difficult matters, or where we are influenced by prejudice. That the reasons we offer in giving rationalizations do not motivate us may be a sign of their failure to justify. It is at least a sign of their failure to convince us; that is one reason we do not like giving them if we can avoid it, and do not like being given such reasons by others in their attempts to convince *us*.[24]

It may be thought that the principle of secular motivation affects only the religious, but it also applies to those who oppose religion in certain ways. The principle is meant to rule out a certain kind of *anti*-religious motivation in coercive sociopolitical action. Democractic societies should be wary not only of religious domination, but also of anti-religious domination. Imagine a scientific argument aimed at excluding creationism from discussion in science courses: the secular considerations it cites might not be motivating, and if the exclusionary policy is proposed on the basis of anti-religious motivation of a kind that does not (in my terms) count as secular, then even if it accords with the rationale principle, offering it does not accord with the motivation principle and does not express civic virtue. Its proponent lacks a set of secular reasons that is *both* evidentially adequate and motivationally sufficient.

Consider, by contrast, a case in which someone promotes a voucher system on the ground that parents, and especially religious ones, should be free to educate their children in academically adequate schools of their choice, including those that teach a particular religion, and so should receive a voucher for each child, which can be used toward the costs of attending any accredited school. Here, the *ground* given for the legislation is not intrinsically religious. One could support a voucher system on this ground without favoring the religious over, say, non-religious people who are simply dissatisfied with the general quality of public education, just as legislators can take account of the religiously based preferences of their constituents *as* their deep-seated preferences without thereby favoring the religious as such over other constituents. This is less far-reaching than government's directly supporting religious as well as secular schools. If, however, pressing for a voucher system is to conform to the principle of secular motivation, then some such secular consideration should be both (normatively) adequate and sufficiently motivating. If my *only* reason for supporting vouchers is to promote the religious devotion of my children, then even if I am expressing a kind of religious virtue, I do not exhibit civic virtue.

The Ethical Significance of Motivation

It should be granted that if there is an *adequate* secular reason for a policy, then no overall harm need be expected from the policy; this is in part why the principle of secular rationale is the more important of the two. In this light, it may be thought that we may offer the reason as justifying our conduct even if it does not motivate us. One may; it is within our rights. But harm can come from the *way* a policy is instituted even if not directly from the policy itself, for instance by manipulating the opposition using rationalizations that do not carry conviction and that may, perhaps in part for this reason, be abandoned by their proponents once they have politically prevailed. Harm certainly can come from habits that allow supporting coercion of others for religious reasons so long as one can find an adequate secular rationalization.

Apply the "Do-unto-others" rule here: one would not like having a different religious group, with which one deeply disagrees, press for its religiously preferred policies solely for religious reasons of its own, even if a good secular reason could be offered. It matters greatly to us *why* people do what they do, and if we have too little sense of it we do not know what to expect from them. To be sure, someone who has both motivating and non-motivating reasons can present both, and this might seem to solve the problem. It does not; indeed, if, in supporting a law or public policy, we present a set of reasons in the usual way, hence without taking special care to imply that none of them need be motivating, the normal presumption is that they are all motivating. We can say, as a paid advocate might, something like, "Here are the arguments," but if we do this in a way that distances us enough from the reasons to rebut the presumption that they motivate us, then in a sense we conceal from others in the discussion *who* we are. There is a place for such concealment, for instance in criminal trials, but it should not be the norm for discussion in a liberal democracy.

Motivation, like justification, is not an all or nothing affair. Suppose one believes that someone with both secular and religious reasons for a policy is not motivated by a secular reason offered. The tendency to disapprove may be modified, if only slightly, where, although the secular reason motivates to *some* degree, it is inessential to determining support for the policies, which would have been promoted in its absence. We are especially likely to disapprove of the dominance of religious motivation if, as with illegally assisting suicide, the policy or law in question is backed by severe punishments. As elsewhere in ethical matters, there can be a wrong way to do the right thing. The right way in cases of coercion must (for additional reasons to be given shortly) incorporate appropriate motivation.

The desirability of having sufficient secular motivation—motivation expressible in terms of natural reasons—for coercion of others supports a distinction that conscientious citizens (among others) should observe: between what we *say* to others and what we *communicate* to them. What we communicate is largely a matter of our voice. We speak with different voices on different occasions, to different audiences, and for different purposes. A soft voice may be soothing, but it may also be threatening; loudly uttering someone's name can express delight, surprise, or indignation. Even when they carry the same content, different voices can bespeak conviction from the heart, the tentativeness of a hypothesis merely proposed for consideration, or the abstractly affirmative character of the detached advocate. It is largely the causal *basis* of what we say, including especially our motivation, and not the *content* of what we say, that yields our voice. Our voice is determined far more by why and how we say what we do than by the content of what we say.[25]

I believe that cultivation of a civic voice is one aspect of following the commandment to love our neighbors in our lives as citizens. One element in civic virtue consists is having and using, often enough, and publicly as well as privately, an appropriate civic voice. Part of civic harmony in a pluralistic democracy consists in enough citizens using that voice as their primary mode of communication in debating issues important for citizens, especially fundamental questions such as abortion, assisted suicide, and vouchers for private education. Being genuinely motivated by the reasons we offer, religious or secular, conduces to sincerity. The perception of such motiva-tion—which careful listeners and readers will often have—conduces to the expectation that one's deeds will accord with one's words. Sincerity is an important element in a civic voice; the expectation that people's deeds will be in conformity with their words is an important element in the civic harmony needed for a well-functioning democracy.

VIII. International Implications of the Framework

I have now sketched conceptions of tolerance—in behavior, in attitude, and as a virtue—of moderate cosmopolitanism as an ethically desirable stance, and of civic virtue. I have also given a partial interpretation of the related commandment to love our neighbors as ourselves and of analogous imperatives appro-priate to civic virtue; and I have defended principles by which religious citizens can balance their quite proper desire to re-alize their religious ideals for their countries and indeed for the wider world and, on the other hand, their obligations to others who differ from them religiously or in some other significant way. The domestic applications of the principles have been widely discussed in the recent literature on religion and poli-tics, but there is presently an acute need to bring clarity and appropriate ethical standards to bear in the international arena. In the interest of brevity, let me concentrate on prob-lems facing the United States and its allies in the Western world.

First, we live in a period of nation-building, a complex and risky process. New nations are emerging; new constitutions are being drafted. Standing constitutions are being challenged. Both separation of church and state and the ethics of citizen-ship for individuals may be more important now than at any time in history.

Second, particularly if we interpret the commandment to love our neighbors in the light of the Good Samaritan story, that commandment calls for much more sharing in international relations than we have so far seen, at least on the part of most of the prosperous nations. I mean not only sharing of material resources, but also giving up a measure of sovereignty in order to strengthen international cooperation. One way to do this is to give more authority to the United Nations, the World Court, the international effort to protect the environment, and other peaceful ventures. A very broad question here is the strength of the obligation of beneficence. In my view, the United States, like other prosperous nations should be more beneficent, enhancing its historical generosity toward other countries and, as peacefully as possible, its opposition to unjust political and economic systems and policies.

Third, there are international applications of the principles and ideals I have proposed, particularly the principle of secular rationale and the ideal of civic voice. There surely is such a thing as civic virtue in the international community, and there is a corresponding civic voice in that realm; these standards have application beyond individual dialogue and political action. A nation may or may not achieve them.

There are also, unfortunately, ways in which coercion can be supported without adequate reasons, religious or secular. Consider the long-standing Palestinian-Israeli controversy. Some Christians and some Israelis think that, through a promise to Abraham, God gave the Jewish people a right to the land now called the West Bank (*Genesis*) and that this is a good reason for Israeli control of, and even settlement in, that territory. Leaving aside the question of just what the promise may be reasonably thought to have meant in geographic, demographic, and political terms, such an appeal to a scriptural narrative is not a good way to determine international policy. It would not be sanctioned by the principle of secular rationale, or any counterpart standard, conceived as applicable internationally; and I do not even see that a religious commitment to the Bible—at least a non-fundamentalist commitment—implies that the appeal would be sanctioned by the principle of religious rationale. A conscientious effort to achieve theoethical equilibrium, together with other considerations, should prevent a literalistic reading of the Bible. The same principles apply, of course, to interpreting the Koran and applying its directives to human affairs.[26] I think we may hope that they can have a constructive influence in encouraging and shaping dialogue among leaders, religious as well as secular, in Islamic and secular nations.

Democracy requires not only legal protections of liberty and of a kind of basic political equality, but also ethical citizenship within the domain of freedom left open by just laws. Here religious citizens should abide by constraints appropriate to their equal status with secular citizens, and the latter should be similarly respectful of the former. The principles set out in this book are intended to guide public discourse and political decisions in civic life. But those principles leave much to our discretion, and tolerance has no substitute. We should be particularly tolerant of those who oppose us but in our best judgment are epistemic peers in the disputed matters. We may also have reason to tolerate both conduct we find repugnant and opposition from those we do not consider peers. In some cases, moreover, tolerance should be combined with, or even replaced by, forgiveness. These points hold for government officials as well as individual citizens; and, in our globalized world, tolerance has international dimensions. But not just any morally objectionable behavior should be tolerated, and some conduct that should be tolerated ought nonetheless to be opposed by peaceable attempts to dissuade. Here the kind of practical wisdom that goes with civic virtue is much needed. We need it to determine both what to tolerate and how to ascertain whether we ourselves presume too much upon the tolerance of others. In all our sociopolitical conduct, moreover, we should try to achieve civic virtue both in what we do and in the normative and motivational reasons for which we do it.

CONCLUSION

We began by exploring the relation between ethics and religion and the status of both as sources of knowledge of right and wrong, and of the good and the bad. Reflection shows that ethics is epistemically autonomous relative to religion. It is, moreover, a domain of possible knowledge. Natural theology, however, is also epistemically autonomous relative to the moral domain, even if not in relation to the realm of value. A particular religion may be expected to draw its moral standards from many sources, including its theology (and possibly natural theology as well), its scriptures, and its surrounding culture, but by no means excluding reflection of a kind possible for moral agents independently of their religious commitments. The multiple sources of ethical standards constitutes one basis on which I have argued for the possibility of theo-ethical equilibrium for at least many religious people who seek it in the right way. I have also suggested that this possibility, and indeed the desirability of realizing it, are consistent with the truth of a moderate divine command ethics. Moral standards may be taken to be both internal to the divine nature and divinely endorsed in such a way that divine commands are ethically paramount in the lives of religious people. But this view is compatible with taking the very same ethical standards to be knowable through natural reason as a capacity common to us all.

If a democracy is to be morally well-grounded, it must protect both the liberty and the basic political equality of its citizens. A robust separation of church and state is needed to meet this requirement. In its minimal form, that separation requires liberty and equality principles, but I have also argued for a neutrality principle as, in the sociopolitical conditions prevalent in most democracies, structurally necessary to ensure the proper functioning of a democratic society.

This book is concerned not just with the kind of constitutional and legal structure a democracy should have, but also with the ethics of citizenship. This is largely a matter of the standards by which individuals conduct themselves in the many aspects of sociopolitical matters wherein they have discretion. In these discretionary matters they have a huge range of options: choices that are neither legally required nor legally prohibited. Within this discretionary category some options are protected by moral rights; and of those, some are praiseworthy, some morally criticizable, and some indifferent. It is intrinsic to a sound democracy that legal rights protect much conduct that is ethically objectionable—the lies, the injustices, the broken promises of many private lives.

Ethics has much wider scope than law. Beyond that, it also calls on us to do more than is required by simply pursuing narrow self-interest within our rights—doing only what we have a right to do and thus avoiding violation of the rights of others. In a pluralistic democracy, even people who do for others far more than this rights-based position requires will tend to do some things that fellow citizens find distasteful. Some of these things may be morally wrong, as with deception of family or friends; but a kind of behavior need not be wrong to evoke aversion. Aversion to the permissible should be leavened by toleration. What kinds of such legally protected or even morally rights-protected wrongs should we tolerate? The law may require us to tolerate certain repugnant exercises of liberty by others, such as many kinds of hate speech, marches in support of racist views, the roar of unmuffled vehicles that degrade the landscape. But in some cases we have both the legal freedom and the moral right to be intolerant. We then must decide whether to exercise that right and, if we do, how to exercise it.

In matters of religion, I have proposed principles both for government and for individuals. Chapter 4 argued for a high degree of tolerance in religious matters. Even where we might have minimally adequate natural reason to institute a coercive law or public policy, it may be best not to do so. And even when a practice, such as hiding the face of women in public, is found objectionable, this may warrant no more than attempts to dissuade rather than oppose in every legal way.

Similar questions arise internationally, whether in international bodies like the United Nations or the European Union, or in the determination of policy by individual nations. Tolerance as a virtue can and should be cultivated at these institutional levels as well as among individuals. The judicious exercise of tolerance does not entail giving up disapproval of rights-protected wrongs, or ceasing to try to change behavior by cogent argumentation. Nor does it entail forgiveness of what is tolerated, though that is often a needed adjunct to toleration and can be essential for civic harmony. But it does require the cultivation of a civic voice. That voice is best achieved when the ethics of citizenship developed in this book is internalized. Those ethical standards should facilitate reasonable decisions in the political realm. They should guide conduct in interpersonal relations. And they should help us both to tolerate the differences that come of individuality expressing itself and to encourage the virtues that, across those differences, we can all hope to possess.

Throughout the book and underlying many of its points is an ethical theory I have here only outlined. But I have noted some major ethical principles—principles of liberty, equality, and neutrality in the sociopolitical realm and, in both the individual and institutional domains, of justice and non-injury, of veracity and fidelity, of beneficence and self-improvement, and of reparation and gratitude—that should have wide acceptance; and I have suggested that these principles can be plausibly taken to be basic and knowable through natural reason. We have seen some reasons to hold that these principles may also be considered acceptable from the point of view of various theological perspectives and certainly from the point of view of natural theology. It also is reasonable to take them as a basis for finding an equilibrium between a religiously grounded ethics and a morality that is epistemically autonomous from religion. That equilibrium merits the status of an aspiration of civic virtue in the religious and, for their secular fellow citizens, a basis of understanding and dialogue with them.

This normative ethical framework makes it possible both to see liberal democracy as morally grounded and to take it to be committed to preserving and even promoting certain human goods. Education is central among these goods. The free pursuit of religion may also be taken to be among them, and the state should solicitously protect that pursuit, but without giving undue preference to it over other peaceful modes of life.

My hope is that the cultivation of civic virtue will be enhanced in both individuals and nations, and that despite threats to safety in many countries (and especially the United States), those feeling threatened by terrorism will not distance themselves further and further from the international community. Civic virtue has an international counterpart, and there are secular as well as religious reasons for an internationalization of the energetic and widespread beneficence called for by the injunction to love our neighbors as ourselves. In fulfilling the obligation of beneficence, whether its motivation is secular or religious or a mix of both kinds of considerations, religious commitment can be an enormous source of motivation; but the most effective efforts to fulfill it call for a cosmopolitan kind of civic virtue in which a plurality of ideals, religious and non-religious, can be balanced in a mutually clarifying dialogue. Democracy is a negotiatory framework. The structure must be kept strong, but we may use building blocks of numerous kinds and may furnish our living space in any way we like. Democratic authority is highly permissive, but it must be exercised to protect this framework. It should be guided by reason, sensitive to faith, motivated by virtue, and leavened by tolerance.

NOTES

Introduction

1. In, e.g., "Intuition, Inference, and Rational Disagreement in Ethics," *Ethical Theory and Moral Practice* 11 (2008), 475–492, and "The Ethics of Belief: Intellectual Responsibility and Rational Disagreement," *Philosophy* 86, 335, 2011, 3–29.

Chapter 1

1. In speaking of basic political equality I refer to a normative status understood in terms of legal rights and political opportunities; there is no implication that democracies should seek to equalize the political power or political influence of citizens: these will vary with differences in ability, circumstance—and socioeconomic position. Liberal democracy seeks to minimize the influence of sheer wealth or of hereditary social position, but the demands of liberty constrain how this may be done. The literature on equality is perhaps nearly as vast as the literature on liberty; and a major question for political philosophy is how to balance the sometimes mutually conflicting demands of each ideal. For wide-ranging discussions bearing on these matters in ways highly pertinent to this book, see, e.g., John Rawls, *A Theory of Justice* (Cambridge: Harvard University Press, 1971), Thomas Nagel, *Equality and Partiality* (Oxford: Oxford University Press, 1991), Gerald Gaus, *Justificatory Liberalism* (Oxford: Oxford University Press, 1996), David Estlund, *Democratic Authority: A Philosophical Framework* (Princeton: Princeton University Press, 2008), and Stephen Macedo, ed., *Deliberative Politics: Essays on Democracy and Disagreement* (Oxford: Oxford University Press, 1999).

2. An indication of various routes—both ethical and non-ethical—to morally grounding democracy is provided in ch. 1 of my

Religious Commitment and Secular Reason (Cambridge: Cambridge University Press, 2000).

3. I presuppose here that there *is* moral knowledge. Do we not know that torturing people is wrong and that one ought to pull a toddler from the path of an onrushing car? This non-skeptical view is not universally accepted. I defend it briefly in ch. 12 of *Epistemology: A Contemporary Introduction to the Theory of Knowledge,* 3rd ed. (New York: Routledge, 2010). Extensive discussion is found in Walter Sinnott-Armstrong and Mark C. Timmons, eds., *Moral Knowledge?* (Oxford: Oxford University Press, 1996) and in Sinnott-Armstrong's *Moral Skepticisms* (Oxford: Oxford University Press, 2006).

4. This view is supported by the different but overlapping conception of the autonomy of ethics given by Charles Larmore in *The Autonomy of Morality* (Cambridge: Cambridge University Press, 2008), esp. ch. 5. Further support is provided in my "Practical Reason and the Status of Moral Obligation," *Canadian Journal of Philosophy,* Supplementary Volume 33 (2010), 197–229.

5. Ross's most important ethical work is *The Right and the Good* (Oxford: Oxford University Press, 1930). The fullest statement of my ethical theory is *The Good in the Right: A Theory of Intuition and Intrinsic Value* (Princeton: Princeton University Press, 2004). Complementary to both is Thomas Nagel's wide-ranging *The View from Nowhere* (Oxford: Oxford University Press, 1986).

6. For a study of some of the empirical evidence pertinent to the ethical influence of religion see Richard Sosis and E. R. Bressler, "Cooperation and Longevity: A Test of the Costly Signaling Theory of Religion," *Cross-Cultural Research* 37, 2 (2003), 211–239. For a wider treatment of related issues in what is now called the cognitive science of religion, see Jeffrey Schloss and Michael Murray, eds., *The Believing Primate: Scientific, Philosophical, and Theological Reflections on the Origin of Religion* (Oxford: Oxford University Press, 2009).

7. The famous ontological argument depends on a definitional equivalence, say of 'God' with 'greatest conceivable being'; I would take this kind of claim to be a philosophical one accessible to natural reason. If it should entail that God exists, the relevance of that fact for this book is treated in ch. 3.

8. Some readers may think here of the story of Abraham and Isaac. I have indicated how one might square this narrative with my ethical theory in "Divine Command Morality and the Autonomy of Ethics," *Faith and Philosophy* 24, 2 (2007), 121–143.

9. This sketchy characterization is not meant to bear much weight, but the discussion of theoethical equilibrium will help to clarify that of reflective equilibrium in general. A crucial element is

consistency between one's general principles and one's intuitions about the concrete cases relevant to judging them: disequilibrium may force, e.g., a revision of a principle or a redescription of a case. An informative recent discussion of the notion is Michael R. DePaul's "Intuitions in Moral Inquiry" (which focuses mainly on reflective equilibrium as involving intuitions), in David Copp, ed., *The Oxford Handbook of Ethical Theory* (Oxford: Oxford University Press, 2006), 595–623.

10. For a detailed and authoritative case for the relevance of the sciences to theological understanding, see James M. Gustafson, *Ethics from a Theocentric Perspective*, vol. 1 (Chicago: University of Chicago Press, 1981).

11. For a high-level but readable presentation of the problem of evil, see William Hasker, *The Triumph of God over Evil* (Grand Rapids: Eerdmans, 2006). I present my own perspective on the problem in ch. 9 of *Rationality and Religious Commitment* (forthcoming from Oxford University Press in 2011).

12. It would not be unqualifiedly impossible, since one might be moral from good fortune rather than from application of one's moral knowledge. I assume, what all but a few radical theists grant, that even if rejection of God can be a moral wrong, it is not the only kind of moral wrong, nor does it make all the others insignificant.

13. I have already cited my *Good in the Right* as arguing for this kind of knowability of moral truths, esp. in ch. 1 and 2. Cf. Robert P. George's point that "Intrinsically intelligible reasons for human choices exist . . . natural law theorists consider friendship, knowledge, critical aesthetic appreciation, and certain other ends as intrinsically 'choiceworthy' . . . The human capacities for reason and freedom are good grounds for affirming human rights, even apart from whether one adverts to a divine source of the moral order." See the statement of his position in "Natural Law, God, and Human Rights," *Journal of Law, Philosophy and Culture* 3, 1 (2009), 132. (This is a précis of his "Natural Law," *Harvard Journal of Law & Public Policy* 31 [2008].)

14. The sketch of divine command ethics provided here draws on my "Divine Command Morality," cited above. I here ignore the case made there for the preferability of identifying moral obligation with *commandability* (roughly, meriting divine command) rather than commandedness, which is a historical property having narrower direct application. This difference is not crucial for the points made here.

15. Note that not all the non-moral properties are non-natural in any narrow sense; consider the religious obligation *to worship God.* Arguably, if this obligation is specifically moral, its basis is natural

properties, such as omniscience, indicating God's grandeur as the worship-demanding kind.

16. This notion of embeddedness is suggested in my initial essay in Robert Audi and Nicholas Wolterstorff, *Religion in the Public Square* (Lanham, MD: Rowman and Littlefield, 1997), n. 21.

17. This formulation indicates how philosophers often take the problem formulated in Plato's *Euthyphro*, but it should be noted that 'holy' is the term some translations use where I have used moral language.

18. This is not uncontroversial, but is defended in detail in ch. 1 and 2 of *The Good in the Right*. But the position that moral properties are grounded in natural ones could probably also be worked out for a theory on which the grounding is empirical and perhaps contingent as well.

Chapter 2

1. The reason for saying they *normally* have this right is that it can be undermined if citizens, even under legitimate government, are manipulated in such a way as to corrupt their intelligence or will.

2. All of these notions are discussed in the literature of political philosophy. For clarification of democratic authority, important recent works are John Rawls, *Political Liberalism* (New York: Columbia University Press, 1993) and Estlund's *Democratic Authority*. Some of my own views on the moral basis of democracy are outlined in "Moral Foundations of Liberal Democracy, Secular Reasons, and Liberal Neutrality Toward the Good," *Notre Dame Journal of Law, Philosophy & Public Policy* 19, 1 (2005), 197–218, which stresses two closely related kinds of evaluative criteria important in political philosophy: *establishment criteria*—standards that enable us to judge whether a *form* of government, such as democracy as opposed to benevolent monarchy, is desirable; and *performance criteria*: standards that, given an *actual* government, enable us to evaluate its performance. This book presupposes the former and, in Chapter 2, concentrates on the latter.

3. John Stuart Mill, *On Liberty* (Indianapolis: Hackett, 1861/1973), pp. 9–10. Mill is strongly opposed to parentalism and (for competent adults) excludes harm to oneself as a ground for interference. See esp. 10 ff. The notion of harm is seriously vague, and both in connection with damaging the environment and in relation to such economic behavior as purchasing goods manufactured by sweatshop labor, questions have arisen regarding just how free we ought to be even if the harm principle is sound so far as it goes. For

instructive recent studies of the scope of moral responsibility and especially of the strength of the obligation not to harm in comparison with that of the obligation to render aid, see Garrett Cullity, *The Moral Demands of Affluence* (Oxford: Oxford University Press, 2004) and Judith Lichtenberg, "Negative Duties, Positive Duties, and the 'New Harms'," *Ethics* 120 (2010), 557–578.

4. Not all public policies are established by legislation. Many are laid down by officials acting as such (and not necessarily within their legal authority). The head of a government agency, e.g., might establish a policy that affects many. Thus, an agency granting scholarships to students might on its own decide that students in religious institutions, or pursuing ecclesiastical degrees, are not eligible for government aid. This would be a kind of coercive policy but not legislated—indeed, it would likely violate the equality and neutrality policies defended in this book.

5. On one view of non-establishment as understood in the U.S. Constitution, the weak form of doctrinal establishment implicit in, say, requiring the Pledge of Allegiance (with its reference to one nation "under God")–which embodies an element of what I call formal establishment–would not be unconstitutional. For a detailed case that such elements of what is sometimes called "civil religion" are not unconstitutional in the United States, see Michael J. Perry, "Religion as a Basis of Law-making? Herein of the Non-establishment of Religion," *Philosophy & Social Criticism* 35, 1–2 (2009), 105–126.

6. My sense is that this is how most English government officials view the matter. As to the role of the established church in England, an article in *The Economist* is quite informative:

> British secularists deplore their country's established church and the national broadcaster's religious programming. But there can hardly be a more comfortable home for an atheist . . . Most satisfyingly for the nonbeliever, politicians live in terror of being seen as righteous. Tony Blair was reticent about his Christianity while in office in order to avoid being thought a "nutter" . . . Yet it would be a mistake to infer from this that religion has no intellectual purchase on British politics. Faith certainly informs some of the Torries' current thinking. Mr Cameron's "compassionate conservatism"—with its professed zeal for fighting poverty and revising civil society—is not merely evocative of Christian ideals in a nebulous sense. It is . . . driven by Christian individuals and organizations (November 28, 2009).

7. The notion of mutilation is of course vague. I do not include ordinary male circumcision, which is required under Jewish and Muslim laws. But permanent disfigurements such as have been perpetrated on female children are mutilations. A democratic state may properly prohibit these. More difficult would be such things as religiously required facial tattooing or other practices that prominently affect appearance and are painful and expensive to reverse. These harms and disfigurements come in degrees; and as in other cases admitting of degree, there may be justification for governmental prohibition in some cases but not others.

8. For a legally informed critical discussion of governmental neutrality toward religion that defends neutrality in a way that supports this essay see, Andrew Koppelman, "Is It Fair to Give Religion Special Treatment," *Illinois Law Review* (2006), 574–604. Cf. Richard W. Garnett, "Assimilation, Toleration, and the State's Interest in the Development of Religious Doctrine," *UCLA Law Review* 51, 1 (2004), 1–59, a wide-ranging informative study of the constitutional and moral issues surrounding the decision.

9. For discussion of this issue see Kent Greenawalt, *Does God Belong in Public Schools?* (Princeton: Princeton University Press, 2005) and my critical study of it, "Religion and Public Education in Constitutional Democracies," *Virginia Law Review* 93, 4 (2007), 1175–1195. One may be reminded here of issues surrounding the "Lemon test": "First, the statute must have a secular legislative purpose; second, its principal or primary effect must be one that neither advances nor inhibits religion; finally, the statute must not foster 'an excessive entanglement with religion.'" See *Lemon v. Kurtzmann* 403 US602 (1971).

10. Eliott Sober uses the term 'theistic evolutionism' for the view that "evolution is God's way of making organisms." See *Evidence and Evolution* (Cambridge: Cambridge University Press, 2008), p. 110. In the main his position in the book is consistent with the view taken here.

11. Neutrality toward a view requires more than avoiding assertions inconsistent with it; it also requires avoiding representing it as implausible. This is not to say that neutrality precludes assessing relevant evidence; but governments—as opposed to individual instructors expressing their own views in courses with adult students—should try to avoid endorsing evidence (or what is plausibly seen as evidence) for, or against, religious views. This point is fruitfully compared with interpretations of the issues surrounding *Hull Church* (393 U.S. at 443), in which the Supreme Court "ruled that the Constitution did not allow the Georgia courts to decide whether the Church had violated its obligation under an implied state-law trust to 'adhere to its tenets of faith . . .' or to 'award church property on the basis of the

interpretation and significance the civil court assigns to . . . church doctrine'." See Garnett, op. cit., 2–3. I see the wisdom of this finding, but suppose the issue were simply whether a particular creed was recited in church services. This is a matter that concerns religion, but a court's finding that a congregation violated a written agreement to recite it at each service would apparently not violate the ruling. The ruling might be described as *meta-religious discourse,* being about religion, but it does not require making any substantive religious judgment. There is no sharp distinction between religious discourse proper, in which content issues should not be decided by secular courts, and meta-religious discourse.

12. At one point Rawls suggests that "the state, at least as concerns constitutional essentials, is not to do anything intended to favor any particular comprehensive view" (*Political Liberalism,* 197). He has characterized comprehensive views as admitting of degrees in scope (13) and makes room for the possibility that a view could be quite comprehensive but not the position of any segment of the population in any particular country. Would this be no "particular" comprehensive view, and might government's supporting it be consistent with his standards? I am leaving open that a view of the good can be highly comprehensive in scope without licensing violations of the liberty, equality, and neutrality principles. Rawls might not agree, nor is it clear how much neutrality in matters of value he would require of democratic government.

13. For an indication of special issues relating to the U.S. Constitution and of some relevant legal literature, see Abner S. Greene, "Why Vouchers Are Unconstitutional, and Why They're Not," *Notre Dame Journal of Law, Ethics & Public Policy* 13, 2 (1999), 397–408.

14. Governmental "earmarks"—funding allocations made with larger appropriation bills—are a different matter. For one thing, they are given to a governmentally selected program (possibly one selected by a single legislator); they may also be awarded apart from any competition; and they need not be restricted in ways that the three separation principles require. Criticism of such funding is provided by Rob Boston in "Egregious Earmarks?," *Church and State* (April 2008), 7–9 (a publication of the organization Americans United for Separation of Church and State).

Chapter 3

1. *Political Liberalism,* 235.

2. Ibid., 247.

3. Rawls, Preface to the paperback ed. of *Political Liberalism* (New York: Columbia University Press, 1995), li–lii. This proviso seems

extremely permissive and raises serious difficulties that I can only sketch here. For a discussion of the proviso offering a narrower reading, see Cristina Lafont, "Religion in the Public Sphere: Remarks on Habermas's Conception of Public Deliberation in Postsecular Societies," *Constellations* 14, 2 (2007), 236–256.

4. See *Religious Convictions and Political Choice* (Oxford: Oxford University Press, 1988), p. 12. This view is refined and defended in Greenawalt's later work, but the kinds of comments that I make here should not be affected by his further work on the topic. Some of the points that I make below are extended or given a wider context in my "Religion and the Ethics of Political Participation," *Ethics* 100, 2 (1990), 386–397.

5. Paul Weithman, *Religion and the Obligations of Citizenship* (Cambridge: Cambridge University Press, 2001), p. 3. This principle is close to one defended in Wolterstorff's essay in Audi and Wolterstorff, op. cit.: "Let citizens use whatever reasons they find appropriate" (112)—with the understanding that their goal is "political justice, not the achievement of one's own interests" (113).

6. This formulation is drawn from my *Religious Commitment*, p. 86, though I published essentially the same version much earlier in "The Separation of Church and State and the Obligations of Citizenship," *Philosophy & Public Affairs* 18, 3 (1989), 259–296. The principle has been widely discussed, e.g. by Wolterstorff, op. cit., Weithman, op. cit., and Christopher J. Eberle in *Religious Convictions in Liberal Politics* (Cambridge: Cambridge University Press, 2002), esp. 84–151, and "Basic Human Worth and Religious Restraint," *Philosophy and Social Criticism* 35, 1–2 (2009), 151–181. In the earlier formulations I used the phrase 'free democracy' since I assumed that a significant degree of freedom is entailed by what I call a (normatively) sound democracy and certainly by a liberal democracy. *Some* minimal political freedom is required for any democracy, but there is no reasonable way to specify a minimal level with exactitude. In any case, the phrase 'free democracy' is not needed here: in a democracy barely deserving the name the principle would still hold, even if the prima facie obligation were weaker than in a liberal democracy.

7. My principle is in the main also less restrictive than one proposed by Jürgen Habermas, "Religion in the Public Square," *European Journal of Philosophy* 14, 1 (2006), 1–25: he says, "[R]eligious citizens must develop an epistemic stance toward the priority that secular reasons enjoy in the political arena" (p. 14), and imposes a "requirement of [secular] translation." His view is briefly discussed later in this chapter.

8. See Nicholas Wolterstorff, "The Paradoxical Role of Coercion in the Theory of Political Liberalism," *Journal of Law, Philosophy and Culture* 1, 1 (2007), p. 144.

9. In ch. 2 of *The Good in the Right* I distinguish different kinds of agreement in a way that clarifies how this tendency to converge on reasons can be present and unrealized; and I have discussed further—generally remediable—considerations that can inhibit the convergence tendency in question in "The Ethics of Belief," cited above.

10. These features are stressed by William P. Alston in *Philosophy of Language* (Englewood Cliffs, NJ: Prentice-Hall, 1964), 88 (I have abbreviated and slightly revised his list). This characterization does not entail that a religion must be theistic, but theistic religions are my main concern, though even in non-theistic religions, the relevant moral code tends to be given a somewhat similar privileged status in relation to appropriate items on this list, such as the worldview, the sacred and profane, and certain rituals, such as marriage. It is noteworthy that in *United States v. Seeger*, 380 US 163 (1965), the Supreme Court ruled that religious belief need not be theistic; but, for reasons that will become increasingly apparent in this chapter and the next, theistic religions raise the most important church-state issues, at least for societies like those in the Western world. For discussion of the significance of *Seeger* in relation to church-state aspects of the foundations of liberalism see Abner S. Greene, "Uncommon Ground," a review essay on John Rawls's *Political Liberalism* and on Ronald Dworkin's *Life's Dominion*, in *George Washington Law Review* 62, no. 4 (1994), 646–673.

11. Cf. a remark by Ahmed Skalkini: "Secularism is often defined as 'indifference to or rejection or exclusion of religion or religious considerations.' Syria defines it differently—not in terms of 'rejection' or even 'tolerance', but in terms of 'embracing' all religions and 'taking pride' in a diverse heritage." See "Syrian Secularism: A Model for the Middle East," *Christian Science Monitor* (July 19, 2010), 35. (Skalkini is described by the *Monitor* as "the spokesman and political advisor for the Syrian Embassy in Washington.") Since his point of view may not be assumed to be neutral, it is interesting to compare a report in *The Economist* (July 17, 2010):

> As members of France's parliament voted to outlaw the public wearing of the *niqab,* the Muslim facial veil that exposes just the eyes, Syria is quietly imposing its own curbs. A number of teachers who wear the *niqab* in school have been transferred to other jobs . . . "The *niqab* is a Wahhabi way of influencing Syria and is a form of violence against women,"

says Bassam Al-Kadi, the outspoken head of the Syrian Wom-
en's Observatory, a lobby that strongly supports the curb.
But some say it is an attack on personal freedom (p. 53).

12. Michael J. Perry, "Liberal Democracy and Religious Morality,"
in Stephen M. Feldman, ed., *Law and Morality: A Critical Anthology*
(New York: New York University Press, 2000), 121 (originally pub-
lished in the *DePaul Law Review*). The quoted words of mine are from
"The Place of Religious Argument in a Free and Democratic Society,"
University of San Diego Law Review 30, 4 (1993), 677–702.

13. I intentionally put the view broadly to accommodate many
proponents and avoid issues not essential here. See Wolterstorff's
contribution to Audi and Wolterstorff, op. cit., for his version of the
view. See Paul Weithman's articulation of the viewed in terms of "reasoned respect" in Weithman, op. cit. Christopher Eberle, like
Weithman and Perry, seems to think my case for the principle of secular rationale depends on conditions for respect due fellow citizens,
whereas I take the principle's contributing to these conditions to be
only one supporting factor. I do not include Greenawalt as holding
the respectful sincerity view because his principle (quoted above)
allowing reliance on religious considerations is carefully restricted to
cases in which "people *reasonably* think that shared premises of justice
and criteria for determining truth cannot resolve critical questions of
fact, fundamental questions of value, or the weighing of competing
benefits and harms" (emphasis added). That they must *reasonably*
think this is a significant restriction over and above the limited, tie-
breaker status the principle has.

14. This is a point with which I believe Perry can agree. With what
appears to be appreciation of the case for the principle of secular
rationale, he suggests, e.g., that in making political choices, citizens

> should forgo reliance on a religious argument about human
> well-being—at least they should be extremely wary of relying
> on such an argument—*unless a secular argument that they
> themselves accept . . . reaches the same conclusion*" (p. 125). He
> adds: "for most religious believers in the United States, and
> probably . . . in other liberal democracies . . . the persuasive-
> ness or soundness of any religious argument depends (or
> should depend) partly on there being at least one secular
> argument . . . that reaches the same conclusion" (126).

15. In characterizing the appropriate kinds of reasons for justifying laws and public policies, political theorists examining or proposing

foundations for liberal democracy have appealed to a number of concepts. Rawls has used the different, though overlapping, terminology of "public reason," and both views (among others addressing the same problem) have been widely examined. Rawls's *Political Liberalism* contains many different characterizations of what he calls public reason. I do not find any single one clear enough to figure in clarifying the position of this book, but it will be clear that on many points my view is compatible with and indeed supports his. For clarifications of Rawls's position on public reason and on religion and politics generally see, Weithman, op. cit., Kent Greenawalt, "What Is Public Reason?" *Journal of Law, Philosophy and Culture* 1, 1 (2007), 79–109, and Samuel Freeman, *Rawls* (New York: Routledge, 2007).

16. Aquinas spoke of "natural reason, whereby we discern what is good and what is bad" (*Summa Theologiae*, Q 91, Art 2). Related to this, he affirms, as the first precept of natural law, that "*good is to be done and promoted, and evil is to be avoided* . . . so that all the things which the practical reason apprehends as man's good belong to the precepts of the natural law under the form of things to be done or avoided" (ST Q 94, art 2). Earlier in the same article he called the precepts of the natural law "self-evident principles."

17. One might question the normal assumption (made here) that a reason, without ceasing to be a reason in any sense, can be a bad one or can be merely motivational; but on that assumption, a merely secular reason can be a reason and normatively bad.

18. We might say, however, that technical reasons are *groundable* in natural reasons: reachable scientifically, by an appropriate inferential route, from natural reasons. The route begins with commonsense observations; these may be taken together with scientific developments that apply and reapply natural reason; and the destination is the technical propositions in question. The technical reasons in question, then, are *indirectly* accessible to natural reason given the kind of process just sketched. Thus, even if they are themselves not properly called natural reasons, appreciating them requires no rational capacity going beyond natural reason, perhaps operating at what may be a high educational level.

19. Here my view differs from from one expressed by former Supreme Court Justice Sandra Day O'Connor. Greenawalt quotes her as saying, "The Pledge is a patriotic exercise, not a religious devotion; 'under God' now lacks real religious significance; the phrase is a kind of 'ceremonial deism' that recognizes the country's religious traditions but does not endorse any particular religion or religion in general." See his *Does God Belong in Public Schools?* (57). It may be true that there is no endorsement of "religion in general" if this

designates an *institutionalized* religion. But there is an endorsement of a theism rich enough to imply that we live under divine sovereignty. Separation of church and state as I conceive it implies—as neutrality toward secular citizens requires— government's not endorsing even minimal theism. For Greenawalt's informative discussion of the status of the Pledge see his *Religion and the Constitution: Establishment and Fairness* (Princeton: Princeton University Press, 2008), 95–102.

20. *Summa Contra Gentiles*, ch. 3, 3 (64).

21. In discussing Aquinas on natural law, Mark C. Murphy endorses and defends what he calls "Aquinas's view that fundamental goods are known through our inclinations, our [natural] tendencies to act purposively to secure certain ends. These 'directednesses' are made intelligible through practical reason's affirming the theses that objects of these inclinations are good." See *Natural Law and Practical Rationality* (Cambridge: Cambridge University Press, 2001), 195. Taken together with Aquinas's point concerning the self-evidence of the precepts of the natural law (among other points of his), this suggests that natural reason is viewed as capable of epistemic independence of theology and religion in basic moral matters. A useful theory that develops the idea of the moral informativeness of our purposive nature is Hugh J. McCann's conative theory of moral judgment. See "Metaethical Reflections on Robert Audi's Moral Intuitionism," in Mark Timmons, John Greco, and Alfred R. Mele, eds., *Rationality and the Good: Critical Essays on the Ethics and Epistemology of Robert Audi* (Oxford: Oxford University Press, 2007).

22. Perry, op. cit., 123–124. The quotation from Dworkin is from his *New York Times Magazine* article, "Life Is Sacred" (May 16, 1993), 36. In his note to the quotation from Dworkin, Perry mentions Dworkin's claim that in the relevant context 'sacred' and 'inviolable' are interchangeable and cites his critique of Dworkin on the sacred in Perry's "The Idea of Human Rights: Four Inquiries" (1998), 145.

23. Jürgen Habermas, "Religion in the Public Square," *European Journal of Philosophy* 14, 1 (2006), 1–25.

24. Habermas, op. cit., 14.

25. I do not say 'translation' because, although it is Habermas's term, I doubt it does justice to the likely less demanding claim he defends. Translation requires equivalence in meaning, a strong condition that is difficult to meet in making the subtle and sometimes cross-categorial changes in question.

26. Two clarifications of the principle of religious rationale. First, such seeking of religiously adequate reasons is appropriate even if the religion in question—as is a bare possibility—does not contain or

imply an ethical view. Second, the notion in question is not captured by the phrase 'religiously adequate reason'. This would vary in meaning depending on the religion. It also too easily suggests a reason adequate from a religious point of view but not evidentially. In using the phrase 'adequate religious reason' I avoid these problems and also acknowledge that a religious reason *can* be justificatory. This is important in meeting the exclusivism charge and in allaying any suspicion that the principle of secular rationale in effect downgrades religious reasons as such to evidentially inadequate considerations.

27. See Michael W. McConnell, "Secular Reason and the Misguided Attempt to Exclude Religious Arguments from Democratic Deliberation," *Journal of Law, Philosophy and Culture* 1, 1 (2007), 159–174 (p. 161).

28. McConnell, op. cit., 169. The term 'prescreening' suggests a rigid rule that would abridge rights of free expression. The prima facie obligation to have adequate secular reasons is (as stressed in this book) compatible with a right to do otherwise.

29. Ibid., 165.

30. *Religious Commitment,* 88. Note too that liberalization may imply what I have called *second-order* coercion: one must, e.g., prevent further enforcement of restrictions by police and others. Authorities like police, however, are already sworn to observe legislative mandates and hence might be seen as directed to lift enforcements as part of their role responsibility rather than as coerced to do so.

31. There is no substitute for practical wisdom in such matters, but at least in pluralistic societies it seems best, other things equal, to avoid appeals to religious, and especially sectarian, considerations. Cf. Jeffrey Stout: "When it comes to expressing religious reasons, it can take a citizen of considerable virtue to avoid even the most obvious pitfalls. I know of no set of rules for getting such matters right. My advice, therefore, is to cultivate the virtues of democratic speech, love justice, and say what you please." See *Democracy and Tradition* (Princeton: Princeton University Press, 2004), 85. Stout's advice suggests what earlier in this chapter I called the *respectful sincerity view.* I indicate some of what is involved in cultivating the virtues he mentions in several parts of this book, esp. the next chapter.

32. The principle of ecclesiastical political neutrality and its counterpart for clergy acting as such in public (rather than simply as individual citizens) are drawn (with minor alteration) from my *Religious Commitment.* The notion of institutional citizenship needs explication, but it is sufficiently clear for its limited purpose here. Granted, it is not self-evident that a church should want to be an institutional

citizen. But even for a church that does not, the principle of ecclesiastical political neutrality expresses a desirable standard.

Chapter 4

1. For a historically important account of the nature and normative basis of tolerance, Pierre Bayle is highly significant. Kristen Irwin quotes him as saying "It is enough that each person consult in good faith and sincerely the lights that God gives him and, upon doing so, that he holds to the idea that seems to him the most reasonable and in conformity with the will of God" and suggests that "Bayle says that God essentially 'lowers the bar' and requires only due diligence in one's search for truth . . . Bayle seems to be separating correct belief from correct action, still recommending both, but with a greater tolerance for wrong belief than for wrong action." See her "Reason & Faith in Bayle's Doctrine of the Erring Conscience" (presented at the Pacific Division of the American philosophical Association in April, 2010).). Further discussion both of what constitutes tolerance and of Bayle's contribution to the topic is provided by Rainer Forst in "Pierre Bayle's Reflexive Theory of Toleration," in Melissa S. Williams and Jeremy Waldron, eds., *Nomos* XLVIII (New York: New York University Press, 2009), 78–113. A related paper that considers John Locke among other historically important writers is Kyle Swan, "Legal Toleration for Belief and Behavior," *History of Political Thought* 31, 1 (Spring 2010), 87–106.

2. The notion of an adjunctive virtue is introduced in Robert Audi and Patrick E. Murphy, "The Many Faces of Integrity," *Business Ethics Quarterly* 16, 1 (2006), 3–21. The idea is that, though not moral virtues, integrity, courage, and other virtues are adjuncts to moral virtue, as where courage enables one to uphold costly moral requirements.

3. Gaus's *Justificatory Liberalism* and Estlund's *Democratic Authority* are good sources of arguments showing the inadequacies of proceduralism as an account of the proper working of democracy.

4. My points about tolerance here are fruitfully compared with many in Rainer Forst, op. cit.

5. This aspect of forgiveness is stressed in Bishop Butler's famous sermons. See J. Butler, Sermons VIII and IX, "Upon Resentment," and "Upon Forgiveness," in *The Works of Joseph Butler,* vol. 2, W. E. Gladstone, ed. (London: Clarendon), 136–167. For extensive discussion of forgiveness see Charles Griswold, *Forgiveness: A Philosophical Exploration* (Cambridge: Cambridge University Press, 2007).

6. Presumably there can also be second-order forgiveness. One spouse might forgive the other for forgiving their miscreant child whom they had agreed was malicious and destructive toward others.

7. One might think that a rational response should be based entirely on how good the argument is. This holds for certain ideal cases, but where the argument is only plausible and not overwhelmingly convincing—which is very common—it matters greatly what kind of person is giving the argument. In part, the question is when we may reasonably allow people to have power over us.

8. The standard in question is also applicable to coercion of belief, as with childhood inculcation or psychological or neurophysiological manipulation. With that in mind a broader formulation would be this:

> If it is not reasonable to consider a disputant epistemically inferior relative to p or less justified than oneself regarding it, then it is not reasonable, and is (prima facie) morally wrong, to coerce that person either to believe p or to perform an action that would be justified only if p is true.

This is from my paper "The Ethics of Belief and the Morality of Action," cited earlier (and a basis of many points in this section).

9. See esp. ch. 2 of Ross, op. cit. To each of these eight obligations there corresponds a principle of prima facie obligation, say the principle that we are prima facie obligated to keep promises. This implies that we ought, all things considered, to do so unless there is a countervailing consideration—at least typically coming from one of the other sources of obligation, say to assist an injury victim. Rossian obligation principles are explicated and defended in ch. 1, 2, and 5 of my *The Good in the Right*.

10. Mill, *On Liberty* (98). He sees, however, a case for illegalizing pimping and public gambling.

11. This question, and especially the ethics of outlawing abortion, are discussed in detail in ch. 7 of my *Religious Commitment*.

12. Examination of the notion of a stakeholder and its relation to the clearer notion of a constituency of an organization is provided in ch. 3 of my *Business Ethics and Ethical Business* (Oxford: Oxford University Press, 2009).

13. Article 18 reads, in part: "Everyone has the right to freedom of thought, conscience and religion; this right includes freedom to change his religion . . . to manifest his religion or belief in teaching, practice, worship and observance." Much has been written on the Declaration, which affirms a rich array of rights. A useful but little

known discussion of its history and philosophical rationale is given in Habib C. Malik, ed., *The Challenge of Human Rights: Charles Malik and the Universal Declaration* (Oxford: Charles Malik Foundation in association with the Centre for Lebanese Studies, 2000).

14. This characterization contrasts with the kind described by Gillian Brock and Harry Brighouse (and attributed to various others), on which "Weak cosmopolitanism just says that there are *some* extranational obligations that have some moral weight. Strong cosmopolitanism, by contrast, claims that . . . there are no society-wide principles of distributive justice that are not also global principles of distributive justice; and that . . . we have no right to use nationality (in contrast with friendship, or familial love) as a trigger for discretionary behavior." See G. Brock and H. Brighouse, *The Political Philosophy of Cosmopolitanism* (Cambridge: Cambridge University Press. 2005), 3. I find both characterizations usefully suggestive; but the first characterization is too indefinite in specifying neither what kinds of obligations are in question nor any limit on their weight, and the second (of strong cosmopolitanism) is indefinite in its first clause and highly vague in its second, negative clause.

15. This view is defended, and the contrast between cosmopolitanism and nationalism is developed in detail, in my "Nationalism, Patriotism, and Cosmopolitanism in an Age of Globalization," *Journal of Ethics* 13 (2009), 365–381.

16. I consider self-realization by one's free choices an element in one's good. But this does not imply that one's good is *simply* such self-realization. This good is thus to be pursued within certain limits. Some are given by rights of others; some are a matter of objectively good and bad elements in life, such as pleasure and pain. This is not the place for a theory of value, but that there is objectivity in matters of value and what sorts of things are valuable in themselves are argued for in my "Intrinsic Value and Reasons for Action," *Southern Journal of Philosophy* 61 Supplement (2003), 30–56; reprinted in T. Horgan and Mark Timmons, eds., *Metaethics after Moore* (Oxford: Oxford University Press, 2006), 79–106.

17. Cf. Philippa Foot's emphasis on desire in relation to the virtue of practical wisdom: "the man who is wise does not merely know *how* to do good things such as looking after his children well, or strengthening someone in trouble, but must also want to do them." See "Virtues and Vices," in Roger Crisp and Michael Slote, eds., *Virtue Ethics* (Oxford: Oxford University Press, 1997), p. 167. For informative and generally supporting discussion of virtue, see Christine Swanton, *Virtue Ethics: A Pluralistic View* (Oxford: Oxford University Press, 2003), and Robert Merrihew Adams, *A Theory of Virtue: Excellence in Being for the Good* (Oxford: Clarendon, 2006).

18. In a certain way, this is answered (at least from the Christian perspective) in the words and deeds of Jesus. But there remains much need to reflect on it. The commandments to love are deeply puzzling.

19. The distinction between obligations of manner—concerning how actions are performed—and of matter, concerning *what* action is required—is introduced and developed in ch. 5 of *The Good in the Right*.

20. Such religious endorsement seems sufficient ground for taking the act in question to be religiously acceptable for those committed to the endorsing authority or set of authorities. But I hesitate to substitute a religious endorsement requirement, since it may be too narrow: we often do not endorse what we would readily approve of on the basis of the very factors that ground our endorsements. We can of course speak of implicit endorsement, but I prefer to take that notion as simply one prima facie indication of religious acceptability.

21. The notion of leveraging and the ethics of engaging it are discussed in more detail in *Religious Commitment*, 109–111.

22. My "Acting from Virtue," *Mind* 104 (1995), 449–471, provides an account of such action which supports the conception of it employed here.

23. I first proposed this principle in "The Separation of Church and State" and have defended it in *Religious Commitment* (the next few paragraphs draw on the second defense). It can be seen as articulating a standard easily justified from the point of view of virtue ethics, but even some who accept a virtue ethics may think it overdemanding.

24. Note that adherence to the principle of secular motivation—even if the adherence itself is partly religious, as it may be owing to, say, acceptance of the "Do-unto-others" rule—may lead a person who is rationalizing (and realizes this) to seek an adequate secular reason that genuinely motivates the same act. If one finds it, the fact that the search for it was in part religiously motivated does nothing to prevent one's now satisfying the motivation principle. There are many routes to finding reasons that are motivating or normatively adequate or both; and the search for either may help in finding the other.

25. Our voice is, however, likely to be also determined *in part* by what we say; and other things equal, a civic voice is not fully achieved if one is proposing religious reasons as grounds for public policy decisions. It may be possible, however, to present such reasons in a context that preserves a certain balance, e.g. by noting that, in addition to sufficient secular reasons for a policy, such as permitting state aid to handicapped children in religious schools, many religious citizens will feel better able to provide for their children services they believe God requires. Thus, the emphasis on achieving a proper civic

voice as part of civic virtue leads to no simple rule about the admissible content of advocacy of laws or public policies.

26. For a treatment of how the Koran and Islamic law bear on democracy, see Andrew F. March, *Islam and Liberal Citizenship* (Oxford: Oxford University Press, 2009).

INDEX

abortion 81, 117, 144, 147, 171n11
Abraham and Isaac 158n8
Adams, Robert Merrihew 172n17
agape love 137
alienation 38
Alston, William P. 165n10
ambiguity (religious) 23–24
animals, protection of 42, 62
Aquinas, St. Thomas 6, 25, 78, 79, 82, 132, 167n16
Aristotle 142
assisted suicide 69, 87, 91, 117, 139, 141
authority
   clerical 78, 82, 94, 101
   cultural-historical 19
   democratic 39, 47, 75, 93, 155
   moral 4, 17, 19–20, 121
   normative 19
   psychological 19
autonomy
   epistemic 11–12
   evidential 11
   Kantian 94
   of ethics 11–13, 25, 33–35, 74, 158n4. *See also* Euthyphro problem

Bayle, Pierre 170n1
Bible, the, 17, 23, 34, 52, 81, 121, 136, 149
Blair, Tony 161
Brighouse, Harry 172n14
Brock, Gillian 172n14
Broome, John ix
Butler, Joseph (Bishop) 170n5

Cameron, David 161
categorical imperative 135. *See also* Kant
Christianity 47, 53, 120–121, 126. *See also Bible, the*; Islam; Judaism; love commandments
citizenship
   ethics of 63, 71–72, 75, 89–90, 117, 142–143, 152–153
   institutional 95–96, 111, 169n32 *See also* virtue, civic
civic virtue. *See* virtue, civic.
civic voice 147–148. *See also* virtue, civic.
civil religion. *See* religion, civil.

clerical virtue. *See* virtue,
   clerical.
coercion 5, 40–41, 60–61, 64,
   68, 74–76, 88, 93–94,
   118–120. *See also* tolerance.
   of belief 171n8
   second-order 169n30
common good 37, 137
comprehensive views of the good
   53, 63–64, 65, 94, 163n12.
cosmopolitanism 129–132, 148,
   172n14
creationism 48, 50, 51, 87,
   144
Crisp, Roger ix, 171n17
Cullity, Garrett 161n3

De Caro, Mario ix
Deem, Michael, ix
defeasibility 13, 14, 66, 132
democratic authority. *See*
   authority, democratic.
democratic power. *See* power,
   democratic.
democracy
   constitutional 7, 31, 111
   liberal 9–10, 45, 53, 65, 73,
      146, 154, 157n1, 160n2
   procedural 66–67, 111,
      170n3
DePaul, Michael R. 159n9
Descartes, Rene 79, 80
discourse
   public 60, 91, 94, 101, 150
   religious 89, 91–93, 101,
      163n11
divine command ethics 4,
   25–36
Dworkin, Gerald 74
Dworkin, Ronald 84–85,
   165n10

Eberle, Christopher ix, 164n6,
   166n13
epistemic peer 117–119
equality principle 40–44, 46,
   50, 55
establishment (of religion),
   43–44, 124, 125, 161n5
   doctrinal 43, 44
   formal 43, 44
Estlund, David 157n1, 160n2,
   170n3
Euthyphro problem 29–30
ethics of citizenship. *See*
   citizenship, ethics of
excusability 68

faith-based initiatives 5, 55
Foot, Philippa 171n17
forgiveness 113–115, 150, 153,
   170n5, 171n6
Forst, Rainer ix, 170nn1,4
freedom
   of expression 59–60,
   of religion 90, 129 *See also*
      liberty principle.
fundamentalism, religious 3,
   149

Garnett, Richard W. ix,
   162nn8,11
Garthoff, Jon, ix
Gaus, Gerald 157n1, 170n3
Genesis 49, 87, 149
George, Robert P. 159n13
Good, common. *See* common
   good.
   neutrality toward 53, 134,
      160n2 *See also* common
      good.
governmental employer
   principle 126

Greco, John 168n21
Green, Abner S. 163n13,
    165n12
Greenawalt, Kent ix, 64,
    162n9, 164n4, 166n13,
    167nn15,19, 168n20
Griswold, Charles 170n5
Gustafson, James M. ix,
    159n10

Habermas, Jürgen 86–89,
    164nn3,7, 168nn23,25
harm 41, 42, 45, 46, 53–54, 62,
    64, 69, 96, 122, 146,
    160n3. See also harm
    principle
harm principle 41, 57, 62, 74,
    103, 122, 123
Hasker, William ix, 159n11
Hooker, Brad ix
Horgan, Terence 172n16
Hull Church 162n11

identity 42–43, 71, 86, 87
individual principles 5
institutional citizenship. See
    citizenship.
institutional principles 5
Immerman, Daniel, ix
Irwin, Kristen 170n1
Islam 16, 17, 53, 121, 131, 139,
    174n26 See also Koran

Jensen, Mark ix
Jesus 136, 173n18
Judaism 16, 49, 53, 121, 131
judiciary 92
justice 63, 64, 66, 93, 100, 121,
    134, 136, 164n5, 172n14
    See also liberal democracy;
    Rawls, John.

justification
    obligating 115–116
    protective 115–116

Kalish, Stephen ix
Kant, Immanuel 130, 135, 142
Kantianism 31, 36, 53, 134, 135
Koppelman, Andrew ix, 160n8
Koran, the 150, 174n26
knowledge, moral. See moral
    knowledge.
Knuuttila, Simo ix

Lafont, Cristina ix, 164n3
Larmore, Charles 158n4
Lawson, Craig ix
Lemon test 162n9
Lemon v Kurtzmann 162n9
Letsas, George, ix
leveraging by reasons 141,
    173n21
liberal democracy 9–10, 45, 53.
    See democracy, liberal
liberalism 70, 165n10.
    See also democracy, liberal
liberalization 93, 94. See also
    democracy, liberal.
liberty principle 40–41, 51, 132
Locke, John 170n1
Lichtenberg, Judith 161n3
love commandments 136–138

Macedo, Stephen 157n1
Malik, Habib C. 172n13
March, Andrew F. 174n26
McCann, Hugh 168n21
McConnell, Michael W. 91–93,
    169n28
McKaughan, Daniel, ix
Mill, John Stuart 41, 45, 122,
    123, 160n3, 170n10

Monti, Paolo ix
moral knowledge 4, 11–15,
    18–20, 25–27, 30–31, 78,
    83, 158n3
Murphy, Mark C. 168n21
Murphy, Patrick E. 170n2
Murray, Michael 158n6

natural reason(s) 6, 7, 15,
    22, 26, 28, 29, 68, 69, 70,
    76–89, 92, 94, 147, 153,
    167nn16,18, 168n4
Nagel, Thomas ix, 157n1,
    158n5
natural law 25, 27, 31, 78,
    83, 84, 159n13, 167n16,
    168n21
natural theology. See theology,
    natural.
Neill, Jeremy, ix
neutrality 5, 45–57, 67, 95–98,
    101, 125–126, 127,
    128, 134, 153, 160n2,
    162nn8,11, 168n19
  attitudinal 50, 106, 108
  behavioral 106, 108
  clerical 97–101
  doctrinal 50
  ecclesiastical 95–96
  political 97–101
  regarding the good 53–54,57
neutrality principle 45–48, 50,
    55, 59, 93, 96, 97

obligation, prima facie 14, 17,
    18, 66, 67
obligation, religious 67, 101,
    159n15. See also
    principle of religious
    rationale.
O'Connor, Sandra Day 167n19

parentalism 160n3
Perl, Caleb, ix
Perry, Michael J. ix, 73–75,
    161n5, 166nn12,13,14,
    168n22
Pilkington, Bryan, ix
physician-assisted suicide. See
    assisted suicide
Plato 160n17
Pledge of Allegiance 81, 99,
    161n5, 167n19, 168n20
pluralism 38, 40, 56, 139
political, notions of the, 98–100
power, democratic. See
    democratic power.
prayer (public) 47, 81, 87, 88,
    113, 123
prima facie obligation. See
    obligation, prima facie.
principle of clerical political
    neutrality 97. See also
    neutrality.
principle of ecclesiastical
    political neutrality 95.
    See also neutrality.
reason, natural. See natural
    reason.
principle of natural reason.
    See principle of secular
    rationale.
principle of rational
    disagreement 118
principle of religious rationale
    89, 90, 103, 139, 140,
    149–150, 168n26
principle of secular motivation
    143–145, 147, 173n24
principle of secular rationale
    65–81, 86–89, 91–93, 97,
    101, 113, 119, 140, 141,
    142, 166nn13,14, 169n26

principle of toleration 119–120
privatization (of religion)
    90–91.
protection of identity principle.
    See identity.
public observances. *See* prayer
public reason. *See* reason,
    public.

Quinn, Philip L. ix

Rationalization 141, 144–145,
    146
Rawls, John 5, 53, 63–64, 66, 70,
    93, 157n1, 160n2, 163n12,
    163–164n3, 165n10,
    167n15
reason, natural. *See* natural
    reason.
reasons
    adequacy of 67–68, 69, 70,
        72, 90, 106, 118,
        168n26
    leveraging by. *See* leveraging
        by reasons
    public 6, 63–64, 167n15
    religious 65, 68–72, 77–78,
        86–102, 140, 146,
        169nn26,30, 173n25
    secular 20, 55, 66–69, 71,
        74–78, 80, 83, 86, 88, 90,
        140, 143, 145–146, 164n7,
        167n17, 173n25. *See also*
        natural reason.
    technical 80, 167n18
reflective equilibrium 20–21,
    159n9. *See also* theoethical
    equilibrium
religion
    civil 6, 44, 81–82, 84,
        161n5

cultural-historical authority
    of 19
definition problem for 72–73
moral authority of 4, 16–19
normative authority of 19
psychological authority of 19
    See also spirituality.
religious argument 93–94,
    166nn12,14
religious experience 28, 32,
    80, 82, 84, 92, 101
    721
religious fundamentalism.
    See fundamentalism,
    religious.
religious liberty. *See* coercion,
    liberalism, liberty
religious obligation. *See*
    obligation, religious.
rights 10, 41, 61–62, 66–67,
    77, 78, 85, 93, 100, 108,
    110–116, 124, 127, 132,
    152–153, 159n13, 169n28,
    171n13
rights-based ethics 66–67
Ross, W.D. 13, 14, 121, 158n5,
    171n9

Sammons, Jack ix
Schloss, Jeffrey 158n6
Schmidt, Thomas ix
science education 48–52
secularism 73
secularity 5, 38, 72–73, 76, 87,
    89–90,
Siep, Ludwig ix
Sober, Elliott 162n10
Sosis, Richard 158n6
Slote, Michael A., 171n17
sovereignty (of God) 48, 49, 81,
    87, 121

Speer, Andreas ix
spirituality 73
Stout, Jeffrey 169n31
Swan, Kyle 170n1
Swanton, Christine 172n17

Tasioulas, John ix
Ten Commandments, 50, 121,
    140
theoethical equilibrium 22, 25,
    102, 150, 151. *See also* civic
    virtue, natural theology,
    reflective equilibrium
theology 9, 12, 18, 19, 21,
    23–25, 49, 78, 121
    natural 15–18, 82–83, 102,
    121, 151, 154. *See also*
    natural law.
Thomas Aquinas. *See* Aquinas
Timmons, Mark C., 158n3,
    168n21, 171n16
tolerance 105–150
    attitudinal, 10, 32, 51
    behavioral 106, 107, 111, 122,
    129, 133
    institutional 111

United States v Seeger 165n10
Universal Declaration of
    Human Rights 92,
    172n13
utilitarianism 53, 135

value neutrality. *See* neutrality
    regarding the good
virtue 62, 170n2, 172n17.
    See also tolerance.
    adjunctive 109
    civic 96, 134–145. *See also*
    love commandments.
    clerical 97
    institutional 111
    moral 108–109
virtue ethics 62. *See also* virtue,
    civic.
vouchers 55–57, 140, 145,
    163n13
Weithman, Paul J. ix, 65,
    164nn5,6, 166nn13,
    15
Wolterstorff, Nicholas 70–71,
    75, 160n16, 164nn5,6,
    165n8, 166n13